Nathanael Emmons, Moses Hemmenway

A discourse concerning the church

In which the several acceptations of the Word are explained and

distinguished

Nathanael Emmons, Moses Hemmenway

A discourse concerning the church
In which the several acceptations of the Word are explained and distinguished

ISBN/EAN: 9783337283636

Printed in Europe, USA, Canada, Australia, Japan

Cover: Foto ©Lupo / pixelio.de

More available books at **www.hansebooks.com**

A DISCOURSE

CONCERNING THE

CHURCH;

IN WHICH THE

SEVERAL ACCEPTATIONS OF THE WORD
ARE EXPLAINED AND DISTINGUISHED;

THE GOSPEL COVENANT DELINEATED:

A RIGHT OF
ADMISSION AND ACCESS TO SPECIAL ORDINANCES,
IN THEIR OUTWARD ADMINISTRATION AND
INWARD EFFICACY,
STATED AND DISCUSSED.

DESIGNED TO
REMOVE THE SCRUPLES AND RECONCILE
THE DIFFERENCES OF CHRISTIANS.

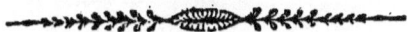

BY MOSES HEMMENWAY, D. D.
PASTOR OF A CONGREGATIONAL CHURCH IN WELLS.

"Prepare the way, take up the stumbling block out of the way of my people."
ISAIAH, lvii. 14.

PRINTED AT BOSTON,
BY I. THOMAS AND E. T. ANDREWS,
FAUST'S STATUE, No. 45, NEWBURY STREET.
MDCCXCII.

CONTENTS.

CHAPTER I.
The CHURCH typified by the HEBREW THEOCRACY—Formed by the NEW COVENANT—Different ACCEPTATIONS of the of the WORD—Different CHARACTERS and PRIVILEGES of its MEMBERS, 5

CHAPTER II.
Of the NEW COVENANT.
Sect. I.—Of the Precepts and Penalties of the Covenant—Who are under its Bond, 10
Sect. II.—Of its Grants and Promises—Visible and invisible Privileges—External and internal Administration, 12
Sect. III.—All in Covenant entitled to special Privileges, 17
Sect. IV.—Connexion of Covenant Duties and Privileges, 19
Sect. V.—Of the Conditions of the Covenant, 22
Sect. VI.—Of visible and invisible Saintship, 26

CHAPTER III.
The RIGHTS and PRIVILEGES of CHURCH MEMBERS, explained and distinguished.
Sect. I.—Communion external and internal—full and partial—passive and active—Twofold Right—Of Admission and Access, 31
Sect. II.—Rights visible and invisible—Real and Seeming—In the sight of God, in the account of Men, 35

CHAPTER IV.
Of the RIGHT of ADMISSION into the CHURCH.
Sect. I.—The Right of Admission distinct from that of Access—Belongs to visible Saints—Visible Holiness a real Qualification—External—Of the visibility of inward Holiness, 37
Sect. II.—The visibility of inward Holiness and the judgment of Charity further considered, 44

CONTENTS.

Sect. III.—*Visible Saints credible Professors of Christianity—What Profession is credible—Of professing saving Faith and Godliness,* 52

Sect. IV.—*Of professing in Moral Sincerity—Whether this gives a Right of Admission,* 65

Sect. V.—*Rule of Admission,* 71

CHAPTER V.
Of the RIGHT of COMING into the CHURCH.

Sect. I.—*The Right of Access Explained—not founded in the reality but evidence of Grace in the view of Conscience—Assurance, certain signs of Grace—Preponderant Probability, and prevailing Persuasion thereof not necessary,* 73

Sect. II.—*All who can profess Christianity unconscious of Hypocrisy or Reserve, have a Right of Access—Conscious Unbelievers and Impenitents may not come—Professors morally sincere have credible Evidence of sanctifying Grace,* 80

Sect. III.—*Whether any may come without an evident or known Right,* 86

CHAPTER VI.
Of the RIGHT of the UNCONVERTED to the PRIVILEGES of EXTERNAL COMMUNION with an INSTITUTED CHURCH.

Sect. I.—*The Question explained and stated—Reasons for the Affirmative,* 90

Sect. II.—*Twelve Objections answered,* 93

Sect. III.—*Reconciling Remarks,* 106

CHAPTER VII.
Of a COVENANT RIGHT to a DIVINE BLESSING in and with the OUTWARD USE of ORDINANCES.

Sect. I.—*A Blessing promised to the right use of Ordinances,* 109

Sect. II.—*Of the Sin and Danger of coming unworthily to the Lord's Supper,* 111

Sect. III.—*Whether the Lord's Supper be a converting Ordinance,* 117

Sect. IV.—*Objections Considered,* 119

A DISCOURSE,

CONCERNING THE

CHURCH, &c.

CHAP. I.

The CHURCH *the* KINGDOM *of* GOD, *typified by the* HEBREW COMMONWEALTH.—*Formed by the* NEW COVENANT.—*Different* ACCEPTATIONS *of the* WORD.—*Different* CHARACTERS *and* PRIVILEGES *of its* MEMBERS.

THE Church is a heavenly theocracy, or kingdom of God, formed by the new covenant; the government of which is in the hands of Christ, who is in a special sense King of Saints. And the new covenant is the rule, according to which this special government of the people of God is administered.

The

The Hebrew commonwealth was a kingdom of God, formed by a special covenant which he made with that people when he brought them out of Egypt. Jehovah was their Law-giver, Judge and King. But this was an earthly theocracy, a kingdom of this world, constituted and governed in this peculiar manner, that it might, as a type, represent the kingdom of heaven, the gospel church.

As all who were interested in the Sinai covenant, which was ratified and sealed by the blood of sacrificed beasts, belonged to the commonwealth of Israel, and were entitled to some at least of its peculiar privileges; so all who are interested in the new-covenant, ratified and sealed by the blood of Christ, belong to the kingdom of heaven, and are members of the church of God.

The covenant then, being the great charter and law of the kingdom of heaven, contains a grant or promise of all those special privileges to which the people of God are entitled, and prescribes all that worship, service and obedience, which they are to render to him. And all who are in the covenant, and so members of the church, are under special bonds and engagements to comply with the duties prescribed to them; and are by a covenant grant entitled to peculiar privileges. But some have a greater interest in the blessings of the covenant than others, and belong to the church in a special and more important sense.

For it is to be observed, that the church is a word which in scripture, and by the common usage of christians, bears several different senses, which should be carefully noticed, explained and distinguished; otherwise we shall be in danger of great confusion and mistake in our conceptions and discourses. These various acceptations, I shall now endeavour to state and define, so far as may be needful to our present design.

I. The *Catholick or Universal Church*, taken in its largest acceptation, includes or comprehends all who are *in any respect* interested in the covenant, so as to be under its bonds, and entitled to any gospel privilege either external or internal, to which others, who are not in covenant, have no right. All who belong to the church in any of those more special acceptations which are to be mentioned and explained, however different in their character and qualifications,

fications, and in the privileges to which they are intitled, are comprehended in this *universal church* above defined, which consequently can be but one. But

II. Sometimes we are to understand by the church, *the whole collective body of true saints*, who shall finally be admitted to the blessedness of the heavenly state. This is commonly termed the *invisible church*, and by the Apostle *the body of Christ*; which in its largest acceptation comprehends all who shall have an inheritance in the kingdom of glory; many of whom may not yet be actual members, but only in the foreknowledge and purpose of God. But in a stricter sense, the invisible or mystical church is that part of the mystical body of Christ which is actually formed; consisting of those who are now the children of God by regeneration and special adoption. Of these some are glorified saints, who are termed the church triumphant. Some are saints conflicting with their enemies on earth, who are the church militant. This collective body constitutes the *universal invisible church*; and being universal it can be but one. It is called invisible, not only because a great part of them being perfected spirits, are removed from human sight, but also because though members of the church militant are visible in their persons, yet those special qualifications and privileges by which they are essentially discriminated from all others, cannot be seen or known by men; and also by way of contradistinction from the *visible church*; which is a

III. *Third* acceptation of the term, the import of which is next to be considered. For it is to be observed that the kingdom of heaven makes an appearance on earth, in persons and societies professing the christian religion, observing its outward ordinances, and exhibiting in their lives its proper effects. And the whole collective body of professed and visible christians, together with their children, are considered as constituting one *universal visible church*. Indeed I do not conceive that the whole number of visible saints are, *by a divine ordinance*, formed into one confociated body. I find no gospel rule or warrant for organizing, and administering a general government over the whole, to which all particular societies and persons professing the christian religion are bound to be subject; or that any general officers are authorized by Christ for any such purpose. In this sense we admit not the notion of a universal visible church, formed by divine institution;

ſtitution; but as a general denomination, by which profeſſed chriſtians, collectively conſidered, may be diſtinguiſhed from the reſt of mankind, we readily admit it. All who credibly profeſs chriſtianity are to be conſidered as belonging to the houſhold of faith; as holy brethren, partakers of the heavenly calling. And ſome ſpecial acts of brotherly fellowſhip ſeem to be due to them; though for want of a convenient opportunity, or for other weighty reaſons, they may not have joined or confederated with any particular chriſtian ſociety. There ſeems to be ſome brotherly relation between all who profeſs the common faith. And ſo all ſuch may be conſidered as compoſing *one viſible church*; which, though not properly an organized body, yet the ſeveral members are to maintain ſome external chriſtian communion with each other. But there is alſo—

IV. *The inſtituted church*, which is plainly diſtinguiſhable from the viſible univerſal church, of which we have ſpoken. An inſtituted church is a viſible ſociety of profeſſed chriſtians (including their children) formed according to the rules of the goſpel, by the mutual confederation of the ſeveral members, either expreſs or at leaſt implicit, for the purpoſe of obſerving the ordinances of worſhip and diſcipline which Chriſt has inſtituted for the edification of the whole body and the ſeveral members, and that the light of the goſpel might be held up to the world by a public profeſſion of faith and obedience, by the reading and preaching of the word; and that its proper influence and effects might be manifeſted and exemplified in the chriſtian and orderly converſation of the members in their ſeveral places. Whether there be any rule or warrant in the goſpel for forming claſſical, provincial, or national churches, by a coaleſcence of ſeveral particular congregations, I ſhall not now enquire. But ſuch ſocieties of profeſſed chriſtians as thoſe above deſcribed, are confeſſedly of divine inſtitution; and in the New Teſtament are commonly termed churches. And their form, order, officers, ordinances and adminiſtrations are preſcribed in the goſpel. An inſtituted church is a part of the *viſible church univerſal*. It is the kingdom of heaven on earth, repreſenting the heavenly theocracy in the place where it is formed. And though chriſtians as members of civil ſocieties are to be ſubject to the lawful authority therein eſtabliſhed, yet as members of a church they are to call no man maſter on earth, but acknowledge Chriſt alone as their Lord and Lawgiver.

V. But

V. But as the members of inflituted churches are not all fit to be admitted to, or use the privileges of full communion, this has occasioned a yet more limited and special meaning of the word: and those members who are in full communion are termed *the church*, in distinction from those who are not communicants. And this *fifth* acceptation of the word is not only common with us, but is thought to be authorised by the Apostles; who in their epistles to churches address them as those whom they supposed to have been communicants at the Lord's supper, and give them directions for a due attendance on that ordinance. But many who are members of a church in a larger sense, are not members of the *communicating church*; nor are to be admitted to the Lord's table without further qualifications. Again,

VI. By the church is sometimes meant those who have a part in the exercise of church authority, a power of voting in the election, dismission, or deposition of officers, in admitting, censuring, or restoring members, and in other church acts. Those who hold the keys of government in the kingdom of heaven may be called, for distinction, the *representative church*; there are great disputes in whose hands this authority is lodged, and to whom it properly belongs, to exercise it. But all agree that not every member is to be admitted to the privilege of voting. When Christ directs his disciples, in case an offending brother will not hearken to more private admonition, to tell it to the church, he seems to mean the representative church, who only have a right publickly and authoritatively to judge and censure offenders. For to what purpose would it be to carry a complaint to any but those who had authority to take cognizance of, and redress the grievance?

From the account which has been given of the church, and the several acceptations in which the word is used, it appears that persons of very different characters and descriptions are members. Some are departed spirits. Some are inhabitants of this world; and of these some are infants; some are adult persons, and of both sexes; some are professors of christianity, others have not yet made a profession of their faith: And of professing christians, some are true saints, and belong both to the invisible and visible church; others are only credible professors; who though regular members of the visible church, are not living members of Christ's mystical body. And of those who belong to the visible church in its largest acceptation, some are not, and some are formed into instituted churches. Some are, and some are not confirmed members, and in full communion. Other differences might be mentioned. But however, they are all subjects of the kingdom of heaven, members of the church, interested in the new covenant,

covenant, entitled to peculiar privileges. They are all (in some sense) holy persons, the children and people of God; and have some union or relation to Christ the head of the church, which those who are out of the church and covenant have not.

CHAP. II.

Of the NEW COVENANT.

THE new covenant is a divine and gracious constitution respecting fallen man, founded in the mediation of Christ, and administered by him, according to which the church is formed, and governed. It contains a law, or rule of duty and obedience, inforced by penalties; and also a grant of special privileges; and establishes a mutual relation and connection between the duties prescribed and the privileges granted to those who are therein interested or concerned.

SECTION I.

Of the preceptive part of the Covenant.

THE preceptive part of the Covenant contains all the laws of Christ, requiring all exercises or acts of piety towards God, of righteousness and benevolence towards men; which are enjoined in the moral law. In addition to these it prescribes what are called evangelical duties, repentance towards God on gospel principles, faith in Christ, doing all in his name, with a due regard to him in all his mediatorial offices, and for those special ends and purposes for which he requires our obedience; with dependance on his grace to assist our endeavours, and his merit and intercession to recommend us and our performances to the divine acceptance. It requires also an observance of all outward ordinances of gospel worship, and an attendance on the instituted means or instrumental duties of religion.

These laws of Christ, are enforced with *penalties*: which are of two kinds, corrective or vindictive. The former are fatherly chastisements, with which the children of God are visited by him for their reformation and profit, when they transgress, and violate

violate their covenant bonds and engagements. In this cafe they are threatned that their iniquity fhall be vifited with the rod. God teftifies his difpleafure by hiding his face from them, fufpending the comforting influences of his fpirit, expofing them to fhame, fubjecting them to the rod of church difcipline, and alfo vifiting them with fore outward afflictions. In fuch ways he chaftens them for tranfgreffing the covenant, though he takes not his loving kindnefs from them.

But there are much more awful and vindictive judgments threatned againft thofe who reject the covenant, and break its bonds in fuch a manner as to cut themfelves off from an intereft in its bleffings, that God will avenge the quarrel of his covenant, not only by deftructive outward judgments, but by giving them up to a blind deluded mind, a reprobate confcience, a hard heart; that the external privileges of the kingdom of heaven fhall be taken from them; and that in the world to come they fhall be punifhed for all their fins, and particularly for rejecting or perfidioufly breaking covenant, by a fentence of final excommunication from the congregation of the faints, and fuffering the pains of the fecond death with hypocrites and unbelievers.

If it be enquired, who are bound to obey the precepts of the gofpel covenant, and whether all fuch may be faid to be *in covenant and under its bonds?*

I anfwer, all to whom the covenant *is propofed* are required and bound to confent to it, accept of it, voluntarily come under its bonds, and fo perform the covenant duties therein prefcribed. It has the authority of a divine law, and needs not our confent to give it a binding force. Some precepts of the gofpel are immediately directed to all to whom the call of the gofpel is fent, and demand prefent obedience. But others are immediately directed to thofe who are in or under the fpecial bond of the covenant, and cannot be regularly obeyed by any but thofe who are firft admitted into the number of God's people, by a reftipulation or confent.

The call of the gofpel requires all who are favoured with it to give a ferious attention to its propofal, to receive the divine teftimony on thofe fufficient evidences with which it is confirmed, and cordially confent to the gracious covenant which it reveals and offers to the children of men. When they have thus taken the bond of the covenant on them, there are further duties immediately injoined; duties which belong not to thofe who are not in covenant while fuch, particularly ufing the fpecial ordinances, which are appropriated exclufively to the church. Briefly then, though the propofals of the covenant are of important concernment to all mankind, efpecially to thofe, who have offers of divine grace made to them, yet a rejected tender of the covenant does not give one an interest in it. And though the call of the gospel lays a bond of duty on all to whom it is sent, yet *the bond of the covenant*, as the expression is commonly understood, properly lies only on those who have come under vows or engagements of obedience, either by their own personal act, or by the restipulation of those who are authorised to act for them. When those who are not under covenant bonds disobey the call of the gospel to them, requiring their consent to its proposal, they are guilty of refusing the covenant. But when those who are under covenant bonds violate them, they are guilty of perfidiously breaking the covenant. A circumstance which inhances their disobedience.

To finish this section. The gospel contains precepts which are immediately directed to, and binding upon the conscience of those who are not in covenant, even all to whom the word of faith is sent. But it has also precepts which prescribe special duties to those who are in covenant, who are under special obligations to perform these and all other covenant duties. And this special obligation arising from their special relation and engagements to God, is, I conceive, what is to be understood by the bond of the covenant.

SECTION II.

Of the Grants or Promises of the Covenant. Its visible and invisible Privileges. Its external and internal Administration.

AS the christian law contains our whole duty, so all the blessings we need are contained in the covenant, grant and promise to the people of God. There are blessings pertaining to the life which now is, and that which is to come. Without attempting to give a detail of particulars, let it suffice to say, the blessings, granted to the church by the covenant, are partly invisible gifts which are connected with, and issue in the salvation of those who receive them; such as a saving union to Christ, pardon of sin, reconciliation to God, and reception into the number of his children by regeneration and adoption, the gift of the holy Spirit to abide with them as a vital principle, by whose influence they are endowed with the graces of sanctification, and made meet to be partakers of the inheritance of the saints. All who receive these gifts and blessings of the covenant are *true saints*, members of the invisible church, and heirs of the kingdom of glory. But there are also outward and visible blessings, of which the new covenant contains a grant or promise. Such are the common gifts of Providence,

idence, and especially spiritual privileges, the word of God, the outward ordinances and instituted means of religion.

But the great question with some is, *who have a right to these external privileges, the grant of which is contained in the covenant?* and whether they belong to all true saints, or to them only—To which I would say, that the new covenant, I conceive, contains no grant or promise claimable by any one till he is first in and under it.

But yet many who are not in covenant, have a lawful and good right not only to receive, possess and use the common blessings of Providence, but also some of those spiritual privileges which the covenant promises and grants to the church. The outward means of conversion, the ordinances appointed for this purpose, and a special blessing to render them effectual, are covenant blessings, promised and granted to the church: Nor have any who are not of the church a *covenant-right* to them; that is, they have no right arising from or founded in a *covenant grant* or promise to them. But yet God in sovereign, unpromised bounty, grants these outward blessings and spiritual privileges to many who are not in covenant; yea, and grants a special blessing with them, whereby they become the effectual means of bringing them into the church and covenant. When the call of the gospel is sent to those who are without, it is not only their right but duty to attend on those ordinances, whether public or private, which are the ordinary means of conversion; such as the reading and hearing of the word, and prayer. And churches of the saints, in which these ordinances are statedly administered, should admit all who desire in an orderly manner to attend on the means of instruction. But it is the church only to whom these ordinances are granted by covenant. God has not promised this privilege to any others; or that he will continue it another day; or that the means of grace shall be blessed for the saving good of those to whom, in uncovenanted favour, they are vouchsafed. The means of conversion *may be* granted to those who are not in covenant. But the church *does* and *shall* enjoy the ordinances. They are a part of its inheritance, secured by a covenant grant. The oracles of God are committed to them: They are the keepers of them. They are the candlesticks in which the light of the gospel is set up, whence it shines abroad in the world. It is in the church alone that the ordinances appointed for the conversion of unbelievers, as well as those which are to be used only by the people of God, are statedly administered. And as these outward means may be granted to those without, so they may be, and we have reason to think usually are blessed for saving good to some wherever they are sent; though this special blessing is an uncovenanted

favor

favor to those who are not of the church. But there are promises that the means of conversion shall be blessed to those who are in the covenant; that God will circumcise their heart, and the heart of their seed to love him: That he will give them a new heart, take away the heart of stone, and give them a heart of flesh: That he will write his laws in their minds and hearts: That he will pour his spirit on their seed, and his blessing on their offspring.—Converting grace is a covenant blessing to those who are in the covenant. And the conversion of such regular church members as may be unconverted (and no doubt there may be many such among the children of the covenant) is the fulfilment of a gracious promise to the church, whereby an uninterrupted succession is preserved therein, chiefly of the natural branches, who are born members. The promise indeed being indefinite, cannot be absolutely claimed for himself by any one in particular; but it shall have its accomplishment within the church: It secures a blessing to them. And hence we find Ephraim pleading his covenant relation to God in prayer for converting grace. Turn thou me and I shall be turned, for thou art the Lord my God.

So that they who are of the church have much the advantage of others. Those invisible blessings of divine grace, pardon, reconciliation to God, sanctification, which are connected with eternal salvation, belong only to those who are in the covenant. They can no otherwise be obtained by any than by admission into the number of God's peculiar people, according to the terms or rules of the gospel. There are also external privileges, to which none but those who are in covenant and of the church may be admitted. There are special ordinances, which others have no right to use, and may not be admitted to them. And though the common means of conversion are not so confined to the church, but that they are also in uncovenanted bounty granted to many others; and though the special blessings of grace are often conveyed to such in the use of these means, as has been said; yet even these common means of conversion are more especially the privilege of the church: To them only are they granted and secured by covenant. It is in the church that these ordinances are ordinarily and statedly used and enjoyed: They are especially designed for the benefit of its members, and the promise of a special blessing to render these means effectual is to them.

But we are not to conceive that all who are in the covenant, and rightful members of the church, according to the gospel rule, are entitled to all the same or equal privileges. Some have a much greater interest, a richer and more valuable inheritance of spiritual blessings conveyed or promised to them than others. All are entitled to some special favors and advantages above the rest

of

of the world. And even those privileges in which those who are not in covenant are allowed to share with them, the church holds by a special and firmer tenure, even a covenant grant or promise. But some are entitled to, and endowed with more ample and important privileges than others. For instance.

Every true saint is undoubtedly interested in the covenant; a member of Christ's mystical body; a partaker of those blessings of divine grace which shall issue in his eternal salvation. But if he has not, or exhibits not such evidence of godliness as the gospel rule makes necessary to give one a right of admission and access to the privileges of outward communion in an instituted church, he has not then a covenant right, nor can regularly or warrantably come, or be admitted to them.

Again, the minor child of a regular member of an instituted church is confessedly in covenant, a member of the church, and according to the gospel rule is a proper subject of baptism, with other special privileges: Yet we have no reason to think that all such children are the subjects of spiritual regeneration, or entitled to the promise of eternal life. And however we may hope charitably concerning individuals, yet they may not be admitted to full communion till they appear to be regularly qualified for it; tho' their right of membership remains, till according to gospel rule they are cut off and uncovenanted.

As every true saint is not entitled, according to the rule of the gospel, to the external privileges which belong to regular members of instituted churches; so the members of instituted churches are not all entitled to the peculiar privileges of true saints. Nor is there a necessary connection, or implication of the respective qualifications, or privileges which according to the covenant belong to each respectively. Tho' all covenant blessings, external and internal, are granted or promised to the church, yet every member is not entitled to all. There are special privileges which belong only to the members of instituted visible churches as such. There are other gospel blessings which belong only to the invisible or mystical church. Though every true saint is in covenant, and of the church; yet many such belong not to any visible instituted church; and so have no right to use the special ordinances which are appropriated to visible saints. And though every visible saint is in covenant, and has a right to special external privileges; yet many such are not *true saints*, and so belong not to the invisible church of true saints, nor are entitled to those special and important benefits which are granted or promised to such alone.

The evangelical charter, which forms the church, contains several articles or branches. Some of the privileges it grants are outward and visible; others are inward and invisible. The former are annexed to outward and visible, the latter to inward and invisible qualifications. And hence, though the church in its general acceptation is but one, yet it is divided into several branches or classes, each of which is distinguished by peculiar characteristic denominations, and has peculiar and appropriate privileges granted to the members of which it is composed. The visible instituted church is distinguished by outward visible qualifications, has an interest in the covenant, in respect of its *outward administration*, and a grant of outward blessings and privileges. The invisible or mystical church is distinguished by inward invisible qualifications, has a more important interest in the covenant in respect of its *inward and invisible administration*, and has a grant of inward and invisible blessings. It is however to be noted, that the invisible and visible church are not wholly diverse in respect of the members of which they are composed, though in respect of their descriptive formal characters, they are distinct. For the invisible and visible church mutually include each other in part: many being at the same time both inward and visible saints; and interested both in the internal and external blessings of the covenant. But there are, besides, many regular church members who are not inward saints, and so not entitled to those blessings which are granted peculiarly to the mystical church. And there is yet a third class consisting of inward, but not visible saints, who are entitled only to internal, but not to external covenant blessings.

Those divines who speak of an outward and inward covenant are not to be understood as suggesting the idea that there are two distinct covenants of grace proposed to mankind. But the gospel covenant contains a grant, promise, or proposal of outward and inward blessings. It contains a rule for the administration of a visible and invisible government over the church and its members. If we speak of the mystical church consisting only of true saints, this is an invisible society; since sanctifying grace, which is the essential distinguishing qualification of all its members, cannot be certainly seen by men. Now the gospel covenant contains grants and promises of spiritual blessings to them; but these blessings are also invisible: no man can certainly know, whether another has received them; and even they who are partakers of them are often doubtful of their own interest therein. But Christ, who knows them that are his, administers an invisible government over his saints according to the rule of the covenant, and dispenses the promised blessings of his grace to all who have a title to them.

But visible instituted churches are societies which may be seen, and distinguished from all others by outward marks, and apparent

rent qualifications. Though it cannot be known who are inwardly sanctified, yet it may be known in whom those evidences of sanctification appear, which the gospel rule requires to qualify for external communion. And the gospel covenant contains rules and ordinances for the administration of an external government in and over visible churches. According to this rule, visible saints who have, and exhibit the signs, expressions and evidences of faith and repentance, which the gospel requires as a qualification for the privileges of external communion: Persons of this description, I say, with their children, are regular and rightful church members; and it is their duty and right to use those ordinances and privileges of instituted churches to which others, not church members, have no right; what these evidences are in particular may be considered in its proper place. But in general we may say that certain evidences of inward sanctification are not necessary, but fallible signs are sufficient, to give one a right of admission, and access to these privileges.

The sum of what has been said is; the privileges granted by the covenant are either internal or external; some of which are in uncovenanted goodness vouchsafed to such as are not in covenant; who have then a lawful right to possess and improve them. But the church alone has a covenant right to, or grant of any of them: And some special privileges belong only to rightful members.—Not every one who has an interest in the covenant is entitled to all its blessings. They are divided to each severally, according to the different qualifications of each one, and according to the interest he has in the covenant.—There is an invisible and a visible government in and over the church, administered according to the gospel covenant, which grants and assigns invisible blessings to true saints, and external privileges to visible saints: The former being in the covenant in respect of its internal, the the latter, in respect of its external administration.

SECTION III.

All in Covenant entitled to special Privileges.

SOME have supposed that persons may be in covenant and yet have no right to any of its privileges. They may be under its bonds, but not be conformed to them, and so not be subjects of the condition.—Now, conformity to the terms of the covenant, it is said, is the thing which gives right to all its benefits; and not merely a being under ties to that conformity. Privileges

vileges are not annexed merely to obligations, but to compliance with obligations.

But I conceive that all who are in covenant, in any proper sense, are not only under its bonds, but invested with its privileges. The covenant forms the church. All who are interested in the one are rightful members of the other. And surely rightful church members have a covenant right to some special privileges above others.

It is true, some who are not in covenant, and so have no covenant right to any of its blessings, may by means of it be laid under the ties of duty to consent and conform to it. This is the case of all the hearers of the gospel: And by having the covenant proposed to them, they are admitted to have and use some valuable privileges. But the obligations they are under are not *the bond of the covenant*, nor are they entitled to any privileges by a covenant grant till they become members of the church. But such bonds of duty as suppose men to be in covenant, have privileges annexed to them: For an interest in the covenant gives a right to privileges, as soon as it lays one under its bonds; and this right is absolute, and not suspended on future conditions. It is impossible for any one to be in the covenant till he has the qualifications necessary in order to his having an interest in it. And these qualifications are all the condition or conformity to the covenant, necessary to give one a right to some privileges. But it does not follow, that because a man is in covenant, and so entitled to some of its blessings, he is therefore entitled to all of them. Many of its grants, and those of the highest importance, may still remain suspended on conditions which have not yet been complied with by some who, yet according to the gospel rule, are rightful members of the church. And though such are under covenant bonds to comply with these further duties or conditions, yet *these bonds* neither give them a right to those further blessings, promised on these conditions, nor is a right thereto any way annexed to them: For conditional grants are not claimable by those who possess not the condition. I am not now enquiring who are rightfully in covenant, and of the church, and what qualifications are required to constitute one a regular member. But that a right of church membership, and a title to special privileges, belongs to all who are in any proper sense in covenant, methinks no intelligent christian, who maturely considers the matter, can or will call in question.

Whenever any by their scandalous wickedness impenitently persisted in, lose their right to all covenant privileges, they are no longer in the covenant, however the ties of duty which they had taken on themselves may yet be binding on them. To speak of of those as being in covenant in some sense, who are by the gospel rule utterly cut off and uncovenanted, is such a departure from the received acceptation of the phrase as is not to be admitted. At this rate we might say that the damned in hell are in covenant, and belong to the kingdom of heaven. Nor is it to be doubted but that Korah, and those who lived in open idolatry, were, so long as they had an interest in the covenant, entitled to some of its special privileges.

Upon the whole, merely a conditional grant of covenant blessings gives no one an interest in the covenant, as the phrase is always understood. Such a conditional grant is made to all men; and it is a matter of great concernment to all ; and is an expression of the mercy of God to the world. In consequence of this, all may be considered as in a salveable state. And we are to love them, to hope and pray, and use means that they may come to the knowledge of the truth, and be saved. And many blessings are daily bestowed on them ; yet we are not to imagine that all are in covenant: Nor does a proposal or offer of this conditional grant, enforced with a divine command, requiring men to consent to and comply with it, give men an interest in the covenant. This indeed brings the blessings of the kingdom of heaven near to them, and even puts them in actual possession of some valuable external privileges granted to the church, viz. the word of God, and the outward means of faith. The preceptive part of the covenant then reaches, and takes hold of, and binds them to obedience ; yet all the hearers of the gospel, are not in the covenant. This is the peculiar privilege of the church and its members. And though all of these have not a title to all covenant blessings, yet they have a present and absolute title granted to them, in and by the covenant to some of its privileges, even such as none but the church can have a regular access to.

SECTION IV.

The Connexion between Covenant Duties and Privileges.

I SHALL now offer some observations on the connexion, relation, and dependance which the duties and privileges of the covenant have the one on the other. The right understanding of this seems to be necessary to our having a just view of the gospel constitution.

Indeed

Indeed the duties and privileges of the covenant cannot be perfectly diftinguifhed from each other. For though there are many bleffings which are not duties, yet all duties are bleffings. They are beftowed upon and wrought in us, as well as done by us. Moral acts or qualifications are effects which may be referred to the fupreme and fubordinate agent; and fo may at the fame time be inftances and expreffions of fpecial divine favour, and alfo of obedience in the fubject to the will of God. It is the doctrine of fcripture that the firft and fecond caufe co-operate in and towards the fame effects. Every good gift is from God, who worketh in us to will and to do of his good pleafure. There is nothing good in us which we have not received from him. By his grace we are what we are. Faith is his gift. And yet it is his commandment that we believe in the name of his Son. Chrift is exalted to give repentance. At the fame time he commands all men every where to repent. All covenant duties, as effects of divine grace according to the promife, are alfo covenant bleffings.

But with refpect to thefe duties and privileges it is obfervable that there is a *connection* between them. Covenant duties have fpecial bleffings annexed to them; and fpecial bleffings lay bonds of duty on thofe who receive them. Thus, that qualification, whatever it be, by which we are favingly united to Chrift, has a chain of privileges connected with it, iffuing in eternal falvation. Thefe privileges are alfo connected with the effential and fundamental virtues and graces required in the gofpel. The habit and principle of thefe is connected with the proper acts and expreffions of them in the life. And thefe expreffions and evidences of inward fanctification are connected with a right to peculiar external privileges: Whence arife fpecial obligations, a compliance with which has further bleffings annexed. Duties qualify for, and entitle to privileges; and privileges qualify for and give a right or warrant to perform duties. But the relation, reference or refpect which the duties and bleffings of the covenant have to each other in this their connection requires to be further confidered.

And in the firft place the order in which they are connected is to be noted. Some are prior, or before others in the order of nature, or of time. Thus in the order of nature the call of the gofpel, accompanied with the influence of the fpirit, is a divine favour going before faving faith. Faith, whether we confider it as a duty, or a gift of God, precedes a faving union to, and intereft in Chrift, and juftification through his redemption and righteoufnefs, with all thofe benefits which accompany or flow from it. The belief of the heart is prefuppofed in the profeffion of the mouth. And profeffion of faith which is a duty, goes before a right of admiſſion to the ſpecial ordinances and privileges of external communion in an inſtituted church. If we confound the proper order in which goſpel duties and bleſſings are connected, we ſhall intirely change the form and ſtructure of the covenant.

It is alſo to be obſerved concerning the duties and benefits of the covenant which are thus connected in their proper order, that thoſe which are before others are conſidered as having ſome kind of cauſality with reſpect to thoſe which are conſequent to them. In other words, the following parts in the ſeries or chain of covenant duties and bleſſings thus linked together, have a neceſſary dependance on the foregoing, and could not be without them. Thus there are ſpecial privileges which are ſuſpended on ſaving faith, viz. a ſaving intereſt in Chriſt, juſtification, the inhabitation of the ſanctifying ſpirit, &c. There are alſo ſpecial external privileges annexed to, and depending upon our having and holding forth credible evidences of faith, ſuch as a right of acceſs and admiſſion to the ordinances of inſtituted churches. But Chriſtians ſeem not fully agreed what term beſt expreſſes this relation between the antecedent duty or qualification, and the conſequent privilege annexed to it; or how the latter depends on the former. Some chuſe to repreſent the qualifications to which the privileges of the covenant are annexed, as *means* by which theſe bleſſings are obtained. But the meaning, as it is explained, is ſo general and indeterminate, that it ſeems to amount to no more than this, that the mean is ſomething without which the end is not obtainable. And indeed Dr. WATTS, ſays expreſsly—" Every fore" going bleſſing may be reckoned in ſome ſenſe as a means with " regard to that which follows."—Others maintain that the goſpel covenant is a conditional grant or promiſe: And that a compliance with covenant duties is the condition or term on which the grant of covenant bleſſing is ſuſpended. This indeed is a word which ſome think not ſo fit to expreſs the qualifications to which bleſſings are annexed in a covenant of rich and free grace; eſpecially as the qualifications themſelves are as free gifts as any others. And beſides, the word itſelf ſeems to admit of as great a latitude in its meaning as the other, in the opinion of the forecited author, who ſays—" Every bleſſing of ſalvation that in the " neceſſary order of nature follows another, may be ſaid to be ſuf" pended on that other as a *condition* without which it ſhall not " be beſtowed."—However, while we diſclaim all pretence to merit in any qualifications wrought in us, or done by us, and acknowledge ourſelves entirely beholden to the free grace of God, and the righteouſneſs of Chriſt for our whole ſalvation, with all the means and qualifications whereby we are made meet for the
inheritance

inheritance of the saints, I see not why our asserting the conditionality of the gospel covenant should be suspected of detracting from the honour due to the grace of God, and the merit, the power and love of our divine Redeemer. And however vague the meaning of the word *condition* may seem, in itself, yet the sense is fixed and determined by the explanation given of it, namely, That act or qualification of the party with whom the covenant is made, by which, according to the tenor of the covenant, the party has a title to, or is interested in the benefits therein granted or promised. In this sense we conceive the new covenant may be termed conditional.

When any one to whom a blessing is conditionally promised has, or complies with, the condition ; then, and not till then, the promise becomes absolute. The blessing is no longer suspended on a future contingency. There is however *something absolute* in favour of mankind granted and secured to them in the covenant of grace, antecedent to their complying with its condition. For it absolutely connects the benefits of divine favour with most gracious conditions, and so puts men into a salvable state, and is a ground of hope concerning them. The grace of the covenant so far extends to all, that favourable terms of salvation are granted to them ; which are also accompanied with various blessings, means and encouragements to repentance. But an interest in the covenant so as to have access to the grace and blessings therein promised, none can obtain till they obtain the conditions or qualifications to which the promises are annexed.

SECTION V.

Of the Condition of the Covenant.

AS the blessings granted or promised in the covenant are manifold and different, of which some have no inseparable or constant connection with others ; so the conditions or qualifications inferring a title thereto are no less different, distinct and separable. It is therefore impossible to determine and state particularly, what is the condition of the covenant, till it be first known, to what particular blessing or privilege the condition enquired for has relation. For one blessing is annexed to one condition, another is suspended on another. Nor can we find, I think, any one act or qualification whatever which has a promise of all covenant blessings ; nor do I find any act of compliance with the requirements of the covenant so indispensably necessary, but that a person may
without

without it have an interest in the covenant, so as to have a right according to the gospel rule to some of its special blessings. If we should say, for instance, that saving faith is the condition; yet it is not to be denied that many who have not faith have an interest in the covenant, and right to some covenant privileges. And there are also some covenant privileges to which many who have faith have not a regular gospel right.

Before we can give a particular answer to the question? What is the condition of the new covenant, we must first understand whether what is enquired for be the condition of entrance or admission into covenant. Or the condition of continuance therein. Or the condition on which a right to some particular covenant blessing is suspended. Or finally the condition of all the promises.

As to the condition of *entering, being received into*, and having an interest in the covenant; it is to be noted that many, even all children of regular church members, are born in and under the covenant, and so have an absolute unconditional grant of some special privileges. Their relation to parents who are entitled to God's gracious promise to them and their children, gives them an interest in the covenant without any act of theirs, as the condition.

Adult persons who are not in covenant can no otherwise be regularly admitted into it, than by their compliance with conditions, or obtaining the special qualifications to which some covenant blessing or privilege is annexed. Whoever is entitled to any covenant promise or grant whatever has an interest in the covenant. And the first act or qualification in any one, which has such a promise or grant annexed, is the condition of entrance into covenant to such a person.

Now as the blessings pertaining to the external and internal administration of the covenant are of a different kind, so the qualifications required in order to our having a right to each of them respectively are no less different.

The first act or qualification which has a promise of the saving grace and blessings of the covenant is, I think, generally held to be a true and living faith, whereby we are united to Christ in whom all the promises are yea and amen. Faith therefore, with a sincere consent, or restipulation agreeable to the covenant proposal, seems to be most properly the condition of access to those blessings which belong to its invisible administration. But faith alone gives no right of admission to the external privileges granted to the members of a visible instituted church.

What then is the condition or qualification required in order to a regular admission and access to these external privileges? This I think is a credible profession or evidence of faith, and consent to the covenant, exhibited without known hypocrisy. Whoever

makes

makes such a profession thereby comes under the bonds, and is invested with a right to the privileges of the covenant so far as to become rightful member of the visible church. He is a visible saint, regularly qualified to come and be admitted to the special outward privileges of the church.

Whenever any one has the condition or qualification which the gospel rule requires in order to an entrance or admission into the covenant, he has then an interest therein, and is absolutely entitled to some of its blessings. There are promises or grants belonging to him, which are no longer suspended on future conditions. But there are also other blessings which are annexed to a compliance with further conditions. Even his *continuance* in covenant, and the prolongation of his right to those privileges to which he is now entitled, depend on his future behaviour. For many have forfeited and lost their interest in the covenant, with all those special privileges which once rightfully belonged to them.

If now it be enquired what is the condition of *abiding* in the covenant, and holding an interest in it, I would observe, that this question is chiefly to be understood as relating to an interest in the covenant in respect of its external administration. For to those who have access to its invisible grace and saving blessings, a permanent continuance in a covenant relation to God is, I conceive, secured by the covenant itself: So that faith by which we become at first entitled to this grace, seems most properly the condition of a permanent title to, and interest in it. But there are also means prescribed in the gospel, a diligent use of which is necessary to our partaking of the grace and blessings of the gospel: And so walking in the commandments and ordinances of the Lord, may be termed the instrumental or secondary conditions, by which we obtain, if not *a title* to, yet a *continued possession* and participation of those blessings of grace of which we became heirs when we first became the children of God by faith in Christ.

But an interest in the covenant in respect to its external privileges, or a right of access and admission to the ordinances, may be lost. And if it be asked upon what condition a visible saint holds his standing in the church and covenant, I conceive it is upon the condition of abiding in a credible profession of christianity, not falling away from, or overthrowing the credibility of it, either by open defection from the faith, or a scandalous life, obstinately and impenitently persisted in, after admonition with other gospel means have been faithfully and patiently used with him, to recover him from the error of his way. Though a professor is guilty of a heinous breach of covenant, if he neglects the duties to which he stands bound, if he falls into gross errors, schisms,

schisms, and scandalous practices; yet these do not, I think, immediately cut him off from the covenant and church: For then the church would have no right to deal with him in a way of discipline: For what have we to do to judge those who are without. The discipline of the church is an ordinance to be administred to none but its members, for the healing of their backslidings. Those who are so spiritually unclean, as to be unfit to communicate in holy ordinances, are yet to be admonished as brethren. The Apostles acknowledged the Jews to be in covenant, notwithstanding the great errors and corruptions into which they had fallen, till they added contumacy to unbelief, resisted and refused the means of repentance, which had been long and patiently used with them, and stoned away, or slew those who would have meekly instructed them, and so rejected the counsel of God against themselves. But not to digress—

There is yet another condition, if it may be so called, which, though no covenant duty, is yet necessary to our continuing in and under the external administration of the covenant, and having a right of external communion; and that is the continuance of our natural life. Death will soon cut us all off from whatever right we have to use gospel ordinances, and dissolve our relation to the visible church. This will indeed be much to the advantage of all true saints, who, upon their dismission from churches in their militant state, will immediately commence members of the church triumphant. But all others will at death be utterly cut off from their interest in the covenant, excommunicated, anathematized, and delivered over to Satan, for the destruction of soul and body in hell.

But after we are in covenant, and so absolutely entitled to some of its blessings, there may yet be further privileges proposed, and promised, our right to which is suspended on further conditions. The question, therefore, concerning the condition of the covenant may be understood of the condition to which particular grants or promises are annexed.

Every true believer has an interest in the invisible grace and blessings of the covenant; yet he has no right to use the ordinances and privileges appropriated to instituted churches, but upon the condition of his exhibiting such a profession and evidence of his faith as the gospel requires in order to his being admitted to them.

Again, every regular member of an instituted church, with his children, has a covenant right to some special outward church privileges; yet if any such member be not a subject of inward sanctification, he can no otherwise obtain those blessings which accompany salvation, but upon the condition of a saving faith.

D And

And after persons have an interest in the external and internal blessings of the covenant, there still may be some special privileges annexed to such conditions as perhaps they have not yet complied with. Every rightful member may not come, or be admitted to full communion, till he has obtained further and special qualifications for it: And there are special promises to eminent exercises of particular graces; for instance, distributing to the necessities of the saints, which belong not to every true believer. And in general, eminent attainments in holiness are the condition of distinguished blessings both in this world and that to come.

But if the condition of the covenant be understood of that qualification which has a covenant grant of all the blessings and privileges contained in all the promises, I must freely own that I know of no one qualification whatever, that has all covenant blessings annexed to it. It is only a diligent, steady and persevering exercise and practice of christian graces and virtues, which will give us access to all the blessings contained in all the promises.

SECTION VI.

That there is a visible and invisible Holiness, which is either Relative or Inherent.

IT may be objected, though it be granted that credible professors of christianity are *visibly* saints, and so are *visibly* members of the church, being *visibly* in the covenant of grace, and have *visibly* a right to covenant privileges, and are accordingly to be admitted to external communion, and regarded and treated as saints by the church, who can only judge by the outward appearance: yet none but those who are the subjects of inward sanctifying grace are *really* saints, or rightful members of the church, or have an interest in the covenant, or a right in the sight of God to any of its privileges. And though the covenant contains a grant of outward privileges, as well as invisible and saving blessings to those who are *really* interested in it, yet neither the one nor the other rightfully belong to any but true saints.

It is here supposed, that none but those who are inwardly sanctified are saints or holy, in any sense, and that a credible profession of christianity, though made without known hypocrisy, constitutes a person a saint only, *visibly, seemingly,* and *in the account of men*. But this, for what I can find, is said without proof; and

is

is an hypothesis, unsupported by scripture, or any good reason. On the contrary, the scripture terms those holy or saints, who cannot with rational probability be judged, to be all the subjects of internal sanctification. Thus the whole congregation of Israel are called an holy people.

Visible churches are holy, and all the members of them, not excepting the infant children. Can it be thought probable that all these are regenerated from the birth? yet they are expressly affirmed to be holy or saints. And is it not accordingly taught and received in the church, that there is a relative and federal holiness which belongs to all church members, entirely diverse and separable from inward sanctification? There are therefore two sorts of persons, who in scripture have the title of saints, and are *really such in their kind*, though in different senses. The one are the subjects of inward and invisible, the other of outward and visible holiness. A visible saint does not mean one who is only a *saint seemingly*, or *in appearance*, though perhaps he may really be no kind of saint. He is *really* a saint, as being a subject of outward and visible holiness, and as having those qualifications which, according to the gospel rule, infer his having really an interest in the covenant, so far as to have a right to external covenant privileges; though perhaps he may not be a subject of that inward and invisible holiness, which is connected with an interest in the inward, invisible and saving blessings of the covenant. Many seem to have been misled by imagining that *a visible saint*, is to be considered as opposed to *a real one*, and so means no more than a *seeming one*. A *visible* faint properly stands opposed to an *invisible* or *inward* one, even as the visible church stands opposed to the invisible. An instituted church is *a real church, a visible society*, formed and constituted according to the rules of the gospel, and is commonly termed *a church*, in the New Testament: Not indeed in the same sense in which the whole collective body of those who are inwardly sanctified, are called *the church*. So a visible faint is *really* as well as *visibly* one in some sense. He is really the subject of some kind of holiness, even that which is visible, external and relative: Though as *real* holiness is often used in contradistinction to the *outward appearance* and marks of inward sanctification, every visible saint, may not be really holy. In a word, since the scripture gives the title of saints to credible professors of christianity and their children, though none will say that they are all the subjects of inward sanctification, I conceive that they are *really saints* in some sense. And to say that they were so termed through a mistaken presumption, that they all were such, even as counterfeit money is called money by those who presume it is good, is only introducing an arbitrary hypothesis, to evade the

plain

plain letter of the scripture, without any necessity, or good reason that yet appears. Men may easily suppose, if they please, *that* none are *in any sense* holy, but those who are inwardly sanctified; *that* there is but one sort of saints spoken of in the scripture; *that* there is but one church, even the mystical; *that* a visible instituted church, as such, is really no church, but only the external shew and appearance of a church. But suppositions are no proofs.

As this notion of the church, the covenant, and saintship, which in effect excludes all but inward saints from a right of membership in the church, and an interest in the covenant in any respect, and which I take to be the capital mistake of the Anabaptists, seems to have been unwarily imbibed by some others. I will endeavour to state and explain my thoughts on this point a little farther.

The word *holy*, especially as used in the Old Testament, and applied to persons and things, expresses their *separation* from common to sacred and divine uses; their special *relation to God*, as being set apart, devoted and dedicated to him, and so belonging to him in a special manner. And as it was required that what was thus dedicated be *clean* or *pure* from defilement; hence the word is also used to express *cleanness* or *purity*. What is *holy* then stands opposed to what is common or profane; and also to what is unclean or polluted.

Hence naturally arose the distinction of *relative* and *inherent* holiness. Persons separated and dedicated to God are termed holy on account of their special relation to him, and his special propriety in them. And as this peculiar relation to God ordinarily took place by means of a covenant which such persons had come under, in which they were devoted to God as his peculiar people; hence this relative holiness is also commonly termed *federal* or *covenant* holiness, which expresses their being thus separated and related to God by their being in and under a covenant dedication to him.

All therefore, who are comprehended in that covenant by which the church is formed, are relatively or federally holy. They are separated from the rest of the world; dedicated to God as his peculiar people; are under special engagements to him, and endowed with special privileges and rights.

But as this covenant has a visible and invisible administration, so there is both a visible and invisible separation, dedication and relation to God according to, and by means of the covenant. Relative federal holiness therefore is *either invisible or visible*. They who cordially consent to the covenant, have an invisible interest in it; are entitled to its invisible grace and blessings; are under an invifible feparation to God ; ftand in an invifible relation to him as his peculiar people, in diftinction from others ; have an invifible adoption into the number of his children ; and an invifible, vital and permanent union to, and communion with Chrift. Thus they have an *invifible federal* holinefs, on which account they are termed *true or real faints* in the moft important fenfe. But as their faintfhip is invifible, it gives them no right according to gofpel rule to any external church privileges. Thefe pertain to the external adminiftration of the covenant, and are granted only to vifible faints.

Now all the fubjects of this *invifible, relative or federal holinefs*, have alfo an *inherent holinefs*, which is inward and invifible. Their hearts are purified from the defilement of fin : They are fanctified thro' the truth ; and fo they are fpiritually clean, through the word which Chrift has fpoken to them, and the renewing of the holy fpirit dwelling in them. On this account alfo they are termed *true faints*, by way of difcrimination from others who are alfo ftiled faints, and are truly fuch in fome fenfe ; though not in the moft important fenfe, as I fhall now proceed to fhew. For,

There is alfo *a vifible holinefs* or faintfhip, and that both relative and inherent, which belongs to thofe who are fo in covenant as to be entitled to thofe external privileges which are granted to regular and rightful members of inftituted churches. Some who are not inwardly fanctified, are yet fo far in covenant, that they are rightful members of the vifible church, as all but the Anibaptifts muft grant. Now fuch are vifibly and externally called, and feparated by and to God from the reft of the world ; openly and profeffedly dedicated to him, they avouching him to be their God and themfelves to be his people. And they are fo far owned by God, that he calls them his people ; externally adopts them ; puts his name upon them ; endows them with fpecial privileges ; gives them his word and ordinances ; all outward means adapted to perfuade and win their hearts to love and fear him, and keep his commandments. Now fuch ftand in a fpecial relation to God as his vifible covenant people. On this account they are termed *holy*, as being the fubjects of an *external federal holinefs*. In this fenfe the congregation of Ifrael are termed an holy people, to whom pertained the adoption and the covenants. And inftituted churches are compofed of vifible faints. And the children of believers are all federally holy.

This external vifible holinefs is not merely a fhew and appearance of fomething whofe exiftence is doubtful ; but it is real in its kind ; though it be of a different kind from that which arifes from an invifible and faving relation to God. And the fcripture scripture speaks of some kind of relative union which even barren branches have to Christ the true vine, though it be not vital and permanent.

There is also what may be termed *an external inherent holiness*, consisting in a profession and conversation conformed visibly to the gospel. Of this the Apostle must be understood to speak when he tells the Thessalonians, Ye are witnesses, and God also how holily and unblameably we behaved ourselves among you who believe. For they could be only witnesses of that external holiness which was visible in his conversation. There is an outward cleanness of the hands, as well as an inward purity of the heart.

Now they who profess faith and consent to the gospel covenant without known hypocrisy, and behave externally, agreeably to the rules of the gospel, are visible saints; and have I conceive, an interest in the covenant not only *visibly*, i. e. *seemingly* and in the account of men, but are truly in it in the sight of God, so far that they have a covenant right of admission and access to the outward ordinances which Christ has instituted and given to his visible churches. This external holiness is the condition or qualification to which the covenant connects a right to these privileges. A visible saint is as truly a member of the visible church, and has a divine right to the visible privileges granted exclusively to it, as an inward saint is a member of the mystical church, and has a divine right to the invisible grace and blessings granted exclusively to it. But these things may hereafter be further discussed.

Will any say, *that* the Apostles did verily believe all the members of christian churches whom they stile saints, to be inward saints? *That* the Apostle Paul, when he says that the children of believers are holy, did positively believe that all such children were, and always to the end of the world would be inwardly sanctified from the womb? *That* Peter, when he told the Jews at the feast of Pentecost that the promise was to them and their children, and afterward told a multitude gathered about them that they were children of the covenant, did really believe that they were all so, in covenant as actually to partake of the saving grace and blessings of it? I, for my part, cannot think that any will say so. If not, I would ask again, whether the Apostles would call those saints, and tell them that the promise of the covenant belonged to them, whom yet they did not believe to be holy in any sense, or to have any real interest in the covenant.

After all, this dispute seems to be in a great measure about words. For let it be supposed *that* the mystical church is the one only church acknowledged in scripture. *That* there is but one sort of saints there spoken of, even saints in heart; *that* these only

only are really in and under the covenant; and *that* societies of professed christians are termed churches only because they appear like, and so are presumed to be of the church mystical. When we have thus adjusted our ideas and stile conformably to this supposition, then we may go on further, and say *that* according to the gospel rule the outward ordinances are not given to the *real* church, and to *real* saints, as such, but *that* all and only those who are *visibly outwardly* and *seemingly* saints and of the church have a right and warrant to come and be admitted. *That* it is not holiness, or an interest in the covenant, but the credible signs thereof, which qualify for this privilege. Thus the qualifications for christian communion will remain the same as before. Visible churches will still be composed of the same characters: *Seeming saints and churches*, will have a divine right to the same privileges, as if they were supposed to be really saints, and churches, and under the external administration of the covenant as before explained. What then is gained by stating things in this manner. Nothing of any importance, that I can see. Only we have laid ourselves under a necessity of putting a strained interpretation on many expressions of scripture, to make them comport with our scheme.

CHAP. III.

The RIGHTS *and* PRIVILEGES *of* CHURCH MEMBERS *explained and distinguished.*

SECTION I.

The subject opened.—Explanations and Distinctions relative to the Privileges and Rights of Church Members.—Several Questions or Cases stated.

THE enquiry concerning a right to the privileges of communion with an instituted christian church has, not without reason, engaged the serious attention of many christians. And notwithstanding what has been offered on the subject, it has been thought by some that further searchings and discoveries were wanted.

That

That this enquiry may be pursued to advantage, the first thing to be attempted is, that the subject be opened, by a just explanation of the rights and privileges in question, and of several terms, phrases and distinctions which occur in discourses on this subject, or which we may hereafter have occasion to make use of.

Communion with an instituted church in the use of gospel ordinances, if taken in its full amplitude and extent, is a complication of several duties and privileges ; some of which are in their nature so distinct, that they may subsist separate and apart from the rest. A person may be interested in the covenant, a rightful member of the church, have a right to some of its peculiar privileges, but not to all. He may be a proper subject, qualified according to the rule of the gospel to come, and be admitted to communion in some special ordinances, but not in all. Yea, he may have a right to attend the administration of an ordinance, and yet not be entitled to the whole benefit and privilege of it.

All who are in covenant, and of the instituted church, have a right to peculiar privileges ; particularly to the ordinances appropriated to the church. But it is to be remembered that this privilege has two parts or branches. *The outward* part belongs to all rightful members in various degrees, according to their several capacities and qualifications. And they are to have external communion with each other, as there is occasion, in a joint use of outward ordinances, with other tokens and expressions of brotherly relation and affection mutually given and received. But the privilege of the ordinances has also an *inward part*, an invisible grace, virtue and blessing in their outward administration and use. And christians have invisible communion in joint exercises of spiritual worship, and cordial charity towards each other ; and in jointly partaking of the blessings of divine grace conveyed in and by the outward use of ordinances to those who worthily attend upon them.

It is also to be noted, that though all members of an instituted church are proper subjects of external communion, yet all such are not entitled to all the privileges of *full communion*. The minor children of church members are also members; and are accordingly to be baptised ; and the church is to express their christian charity towards them by receiving them as belonging to Christ, interested in the covenant, as the children of God, at least by external adoption, as federally holy, and as those concerning whom there are special reasons to hope that they either are, or will be inwardly sanctified. They are the special objects of the inspection, prayers and benedictions of the church ; and care is to be taken that they be brought up in the nurture and admonition of the Lord.

Lord. And as they advance to adult age, they have the special privilege of being under the watch and discipline of the church and the dispensation of the word and ordinances of God. This right of membership, with the external privileges thereto annexed, belongs to the children of all members who are not so scandalous as justly to forfeit, and lose their standing in the church.*

But infant members, are not qualified, and have not a right to come, and be admitted to the Lord's supper, and the special privileges of full communion. And this too, I conceive, may be the case with some adult members. They may labour under so much ignorance and mistake, particularly as to the nature and design of this ordinance and the qualifications for it, as that they cannot come to it without wounding their conscience. They may think that none can warrantably come, unless they have more certain evidence of inward sanctification than they have yet attained to. Mistakes like this have probably kept many back, whose right of membership was unquestionable; who abide in a credible profession of the christian religion, joined with an unblameable conversation, and are hopefully persons of christian piety. While one is under a mistake of this kind, he cannot in faith take the standing and privileges of a member in full communion; how much soever his profession and practice may commend him to the charity of others; and how good reasons soever he may have of the hope that is in him. And I find no warrant in the gospel to excommunicate a rightful church member, a serious and credible professor of an unblameable life, because he has not such undoubting confidence in his own fitness to come to the table of the Lord, as he perhaps through mistake thinks would be necessary to warrant his so doing. Such therefore must, I think, be allowed to be rightful members, and as such entitled to special church privileges; though the scruples, doubts and mistakes they labour under unfit them for the privilege of full communion. Therefore though we have no concern with the *half-way covenant*, which

some

---

* Some have thought that no adult persons are to be accounted church members unless they come into full communion. But our churches have always been generally of a different judgment; admitting those who profess faith, and a consent to the covenant, to some privileges of external communion for themselves and children, though they should not come to the Lord's supper. The reasons on which their judgment and practice are grounded may be seen in the result of the synod at Boston in the year 1662. Which are more largely discussed and defended by Mr. John Allen, Mr. Richard Mather, Mr. Jonathan Mitchel. Whose arguments I think have never been well answered, and I see not how they can be.

some talk of, yet we dare not refuse to admit to *partial communion* orderly and rightful members, though by reason of their doubts or mistakes they should not appear actually fit to come to the Lord's supper to their comfort and edification.

But without discussing this point, it is supposed that some who have not a right of actual fitness for full communion may, as rightful members, be proper subjects of *some* special church privileges. But there are some further special external privileges which belong to members in full communion: Some ordinances, to which such only may come and be admitted; particularly the Lord's supper, and giving their suffrage with the church in acts of government and discipline, (not to mention the peculiar privileges of public officers.) Members of this class are not only to be respected, loved and treated as disciples of Christ in charitable account, but also as more confirmed and perfect members in spiritual attainments.

These observations shew that the subject proposed to examination involves several distinct cases which will require to be discussed separately.

First, Who are qualified according to the rule of the gospel to be members of an instituted church?

Secondly, Who are qualified for, and have a right to the privileges of full external communion?

Thirdly, Who have a covenant right to the inward special blessing of Christ, and the sanctifying virtue and efficacy of the ordinances, in and with the outward administration and use of them?

It is further to be observed, that the external communion, which church members have with each other in gospel ordinances, is either *active* or *passive*. When we voluntarily come and join with the church in using special ordinances, we have *active communion* with them. But they who are only passive subjects to whom special ordinances or privileges are applied, as in the administration of baptism to infants, these have *passive communion*. And this is also the case when any one is admitted into the church, or to any special privilege; for admission is not the act of the person admitted, but of those who admit him.

Hence the right of external communion with an instituted church consists of two parts or branches. First, the right of *passive communion*, or of *being admitted* as fit subjects to whom special ordinances are to be administered, or on whom special external privileges are to be conferred. This we shall for distinction call *a right of admission*; or a *title* to the privilege of being admitted, regarded, and treated by the church as a proper subject of

external

external communion. The other branch is *a right of active communion*; of coming voluntarily into the church, of using the special ordinances and privileges which belong only to its members. And this we may call *a right of access*, or *a warrant* to come, to ask for, actively receive, and use these privileges.

A *title to admission*, and a *warrant for coming* are very different: They are annexed to different qualifications, and stand on different grounds. A person whose right of admission is clear and unexceptionable may have no right or warrant at all to come for, or use the privileges of a rightful member. Though a right of admission and of access are both required to give one *a full* and *regular right* to the privilege of external communion, yet they must by no means be confounded together: but considered and determined separately by their proper rules and measures. I shall therefore in discussing the right of external communion, enquire first who have a right to be admitted, and then who have a right to come.

SECTION XI.

Other Distinctions considered.

BESIDES these distinctions, which we have proposed for the purpose of reducing the several branches of this complicated subject to a proper train and method, that so each part may be examined without confusion; there are several others to be met with in the discourses of those who have treated on this argument: Such as a *visible right*, a right in *the sight or account of men*, contradistinguished from *a right in sight of God*.

On this I would observe. That the gospel is the rule by which all rights to, or claims of spiritual privileges are to be tried. If we judge according to this rule, as we ought to do, no rights can be visible to us but such as are real. Nonentities are not visible objects. Whatever is visible either to the bodily or mental eye is certainly real, unless our eyes are in fault, and create their own objects.

A *visible right* then is not to be opposed to a *real one*, or considered as of doubtful validity. It is founded in *reality*. It is by the rule of the gospel annexed to certain qualifications which may be seen by men. As far as it goes, it is as firm as the covenant of grace, on which it is founded. It properly stands opposed only to *those rights which are invisible* to men, and are not within their view and cognizance.

It

It is only the *right of admission* which is *visible* to the church, or of which they have a warrant to judge. And this belongs *really* to all whom the church ought to receive, be their inward character and qualifications what they may. Whether such have *a right to come*, and actively take and use the privilege of members, the church knows not. They cannot discern those inward qualifications to which the right of access is annexed. The door keepers of the church are bound not to debar any from external communion who have this *visible right*, this *right of admission*; but receive them as christian brethren in charitable account. And though the rule of the gospel should be plainly laid before those who offer themselves for admission to special privileges, and it is the duty of spiritual guides to assist them in examining themselves, yet it must be left to every man's conscience to determine, whether he has a good warrant to take and use those privileges to which he may be admitted.

A visible right to church privileges in the sight of men, judging according to the rule of the gospel, is therefore not a mere *seeming right*, or an appearance of doubtful reality. It is valid in the sight of God. The act of a church regularly receiving to communion those who have a visible right, is ratified by Christ himself, who says, Suffer such to come, and forbid them not. Whosoever receiveth such in my name receiveth me.

But it is to be remembered that a visible right, though real and valid in the sight of God and man, yet is no *warrant* for any one *actively to take and use any of the special ordinances or privileges of the church*. It is not a *full* and *absolute* right to them. It is only one branch. The other lies out of the sight of the church, and is to be examined and approved in the court of conscience. He who has a visible right, may indeed claim the privilege of having the doors of the church open to receive him, and upon his coming in, he is a proper subject of passive communion, that is, to be received and regarded as a faithful brother. But if he has not also a right arising from inward qualifications, which no man can discern in another, he can have no lawful access actively to take and use the privileges of a member.

Upon the whole; if any by a visible right to privileges mean no more than a *seeming one*, this ought to be of no more account with men, than it is in the sight of God. A nullity will be regarded as such, if it be judged of according to the rule. If by a visible right be meant *a right connected with qualifications discernable by men*, which seems to be the most proper acceptation; this, as far as it goes, is as real and valid in the sight of God, as it ought to be in the account of men. The subject is, in the just

account

account of the church, and by the sentence of God himself, entitled to admission to external communion. Finally, if, by a right in the sight of God, be meant a *full and absolute right to privileges* to use as well as be admitted to them, this none have *in the sight of the church*, which pretends not to discern those inward qualifications which are necessary to give one this right. In a word, though christians may, in the sight of God, have a covenant right to important privileges, which the church cannot discern, yet I conceive that there is no visible right which any one has in the just account of men, which is not as good and valid in the sight of God. Perhaps the loose way in which some use this distinction, of a visible right in the sight of men, and real right in the sight of God, may have led some unwarily to imagine, that the church can act only in an uncertain, conjectural manner, in judging who are entitled to external privileges, which is, I think, a mistake, tending to fill the minds of christians with scruples, and entangle them in inextricable perplexities. But if they attend to the rule of the gospel, and regulate their judgment concerning the visible rights of proponants by it, they need not doubt but that whatsoever they bind on earth is bound in heaven, and whatsoever they loose on earth is loosed in heaven.

Having endeavoured, in the preceding remarks, to give some general opening to the subject, I shall next proceed to consider the several cases mentioned in their order.

CHAP. IV.

Of the RIGHT *of* ADMISSION *into the* CHURCH.

SECTION I.

The Right of Admission distinct from the Right of Access.—Visible Saints the Subjects of it.—External Holiness only properly Visible.—In what Sense inward Holiness may be said to be Visible.

THE enquiry now to be especially attended to is, who have a *right of admission* into the church; who are qualified to have some at least of the special outward privileges of church members conferred upon them?

The right of admission now enquired for, evidently means not the *right of admitting* into the church. It belongs to the church in subordination to Christ, ministerially and declaratorily in his name, to admit or reject those who offer themselves. But it is *the right of being admitted to external communion*, or of having special privileges conferred upon one, of which we are considering who are rightful subjects.

Since admission in this sense is not the act of the person admitted, but a passive reception of a privilege; the right in question is not a right to act, or do any thing, but to have a benefit conferred. Indeed, no adult person can ordinarily become a member of a church without his own concurring act. And his being admitted is not sufficient to constitute him a rightful member, unless he has a right to do his part in concurrence with the church. But this will be considered in its proper place.

Now there is an important difference between a right to act, and a right passively to receive or be admitted to a privilege. A right to receive, or possess a privilege, is the same with *a title* to it. But a right to act is *a warrant* for doing it. A man may have a good title to privileges, though he neither knows nor believes any thing of it. But no one can have a warrant to act which will justify him without being conscious of it? All true saints have a covenant title to the privileges of the children of God, though some doubt of it, and believe it not. But no one can have a sufficient warrant for doing any thing while he thinks he has not. *Our title* to any benefit is not at all invalidated, if we are ever so fully persuaded that it belongs not to us. But *a warrant or right to act* must be approved in the court of conscience.

Our *title* to gospel privileges is founded in the grant or promise of the new covenant to persons qualified, whether we are conscious of having these qualifications or not. But *a warrant or right to act* arises from, and is always annexed to a sufficient reason for acting in the judgment of our own conscience, when rightly informed. If then it be asked, who have a right to be admitted to external communion with an instituted church, the answer must be, they who have the qualifications to which, according to the gospel, a *title* to the privilege of admission is annexed. But if it be asked, who have a right or warrant to come into the church, and take and use the privileges of external communion, the answer will be, they who have *sufficient reasons* so to do, in the judgment of their own conscience when rightly informed.

It is the first of these enquiries which is now to be attended to. In answer to which, I would say in general: All and only they whom the church, by the rule of the gospel, may and ought to receive, have a right of admission. And all ought to be received

who

who exhibit sufficient evidence that they are qualified for it. And I take it for granted by all, that visible saints exhibit sufficient evidence of this, and so have a right of admission, except something scandalous should appear in them, for which they ought to be debarred.*

I shall not now enquire, what causes may be thought sufficient to bar a visible saint of his right of admission. But shall confine my attention chiefly to this which seems to be the main question. Who are visible saints? On which I would observe,

A visible saint is a subject of that holiness, or saintship, *which may be seen or discerned by the church.* He is not only a visible person who is a saint, but it may be seen that he is a saint. This is not only visible to God, and his own conscience, but also to his fellow christians.

We may here take notice, that *that* holiness which forms the character in question is a visible qualification. It may be discerned in another by a due use of human faculties. But here two enquiries occur, which will require a careful attention. *What is that holiness* which is thus visible? And *what is the visibility* here supposed? or, in what sense may it be seen?

It has already been observed, that there are two sorts of persons, whose real characters are often very different, who are in scripture termed saints; and that there are two kinds of holiness, which give them this denomination. There is an internal and an external covenant dedication to God. An inward purity of heart, and an outward sanctity exhibited in words and behaviour. The one sort are saints outwardly, the other are saints inwardly. This distinction is authorised by the Apostle. "He is not a Jew, who is one outwardly; neither is that circumcision which is outward in the flesh: But he is a Jew who is one inwardly, and circumcision

---

* This limitation seems necessary. Visible saints may be so ignorant, or erroneous, or disorderly in their conversation, as to be unfit to have active communion with a church in special ordinances, till they are cleansed from these stains and defilements. It is not every blemish in a man's character which disqualifies for admission into the church. Nor can it be concluded that a man is not a visible saint merely from his being scandalous, so as to be at present unfit to be admitted to communion. There may be manifest evidences of real saintship, notwithstanding, and rational and scriptural grounds for charity. We are not bound to admit all to communion for whom we may and ought to exercise charity. Though none should be admitted but such as are saints in the just account of the church, yet some who are to be reputed saints, may yet be justly debarred. The door of the visible church is indeed so wide that many have a right to be admitted, who will be excluded from the church in heaven. And I trust that the gate of heaven is also so wide, that some will be received into those blissful mansions who were unfit to be received to external communion with an instituted church.

cifion is that of the heart." The Jews were faints, or a holy people *outwardly* and in the letter; and as fuch were the fubjects of the outward circumcifion, with the other outward ordinances, and privileges of the church under the Old Teftament. But they only were the fpiritual feed of Abraham, a holy people, in that more important fenfe which the Apoftle has in view, who were Jews inwardly, and circumcifed in heart. Now fince external and internal holinefs are different qualifications, and an outward and an inward faint are different characters, the queftion is, what kind of holinefs muft be vifible to the church in any one, to denominate him a vifible faint? Is it external, or internal faintfhip, which muft be *vifible*, to give him a right of admiffion?

But before we proceed to the refolution of this point, it will be needful to explain and ftate what we mean by the *vifibility* of holinefs or faintfhip: Or in what fenfe, the qualifications which form and difcriminate the character of a vifible faint *may be feen*.

An object is faid to be vifible in the ftricteft fenfe when it may be feen, or perceived by the eye. But as we commonly exprefs the faculties, acts or operations of the mind in terms and phrafes borrowed from bodily and fenfible things, fo things are faid to be vifible to the mind, when they may in any way be difcerned or known by us. And the feveral inlets of the mind thro' which it receives its information are figuratively termed the *eyes* of the mind, by which it *fees* objects. Senfible objects are faid to be vifible to the *eye of fenfe*. Some truths are immediately vifible, or felf-evident to the *eye of the mind* as foon as they are clearly underftood. Some truths are vifible to the *eye of reafon*, as being demonftrable from the difcernable connection they have with fome known truth. Thus the being of the invifible God may be *clearly feen* from the works of creation. Some truths are vifible to the *eye of faith*, being confirmed by the teftimony of God. Thus Abraham by faith *faw* the day of Chrift afar off, and was glad. But let it be obferved, that nothing is vifible, properly fpeaking, but what is true and real. That which is not, cannot be feen, either immediately, or by means of any fure connection, with any other truth. If the evidence we have of the exiftence of any thing leaves it doubtful whether the thing fuppofed has any exiftence, if we can only form a conjectural opinion from it, it would be, I think, a harfh catachrefis to fay that it was an object that could be feen by us. If we have not light enough to afcertain the reality of a fuppofed object, there is not enough, to make it vifible.

Now, if nothing be vifible, but what may be feen, and if nothing can be feen, unlefs there be light enough to afcertain its reality; it feems to be at leaft an improper way of fpeaking to oppofe

a vifible

a visible saint to a real one, as was before observed. How that can be seen which is not, or whose reality cannot be discerned, I understand not.

But if a visible saint be one who may be seen to be a saint, if visible holiness be holiness which may be seen, and whose reality may be ascertained, it is evident that it is external, and not internal holiness which forms the character of a visible saint, as such. It is the visibility of this, and not of inward sanctification, which gives a right of admission into the church.

For it is external holiness alone which is visible, according to the explanation which has been given: Holiness of heart is an invisible qualification, as is generally taught in the reformed churches. It is the ornament of the hidden man of the heart: A new name, which no man knoweth but he who receiveth it: It can be seen by him only who can search the heart. It cannot be discerned in another by the eye of sense, by immediate intuition, by reason, or by faith. Its reality cannot be made visible, or ascertained by any evidence we can have access to. It has not a known, and certain connection with any thing discernable by us.

Now, if inward holiness be not visible to the eye of man; then it cannot be the visibility of this which gives any one the title of a visible saint, and a right of admission. Nor is there any such character as a *visible saint in heart*. To speak of one as being visibly, that is, outwardly gracious, circumcised in heart, seems to be as improper, as it would be to say that he was visibly possest of an invisible qualification. It must be the visibility of that holiness which is visible, that is, of external holiness, which denominates a visible saint, and qualifies for admission to external church communion.

Some have thought that there is but one sort of holiness, or saints spoken of in scripture.* But if there be any such character as a visible saint, if that holiness which forms this character, be a visible qualification; on the contrary, if that which forms the character of a saint in heart is not a visible qualification, I see not how it can be denied that there are two kinds of holiness, and saints. If the scripture gives the title of saints to some who are not saints in heart, and if the scriptures do not give titles to any which do not belong to them; then there are two sorts of persons to whom the title of saints truly belongs. Indeed we are apt enough to miscall things through ignorance or mistake; but the holy Spirit, by whose inspiration the scriptures were given, is not subject to our weaknesses.

A visible saint is a real definite character, essentially different from that of a saint in heart. And such are entitled to some

* It might as well have been said, that one sort of Jews only was spoken of, and one kind of circumcision, even that of the heart.

special privileges, to which a saint in heart, as such, is not admissible. It is true, these different characters often meet in the same subject; but they often are also separated. And an outward saint is as really a saint in his kind, as an inward one. The unregenerate child of a believer is as really a subject of external federal holiness, as the believer himself is of inward sanctifying grace; and the one is as rightful a member of the visible, as the other is of the invisible church.

In short, if the notion of visibility has been rightly stated, if nothing is visible but what can be seen, and nothing can be seen unless there be light or evidence enough to ascertain its real existence; it seems plain that it is not inward, but outward holiness which can be seen in another, and which denominates him a visible saint.

Here it may probably be said, that a thing may be said to be visible, in some sense, if it appear *probable*, or *credible*, though there should be no certainty of its reality. And that grace may be said to be *visible* in this sense. There may be evidence sufficient to make it *visible to the eye or judgment of rational charity*, that a person is a saint in heart, though it be not sufficient to make it certain that he is really such a one. And it is the visibility of inward sanctification to the eye of charity, by the light of probable, though uncertain evidence, which gives one the denomination of a visible saint: So that the holiness supposed is holiness of heart. But its being visible, does not mean that it can certainly be seen or known to be real, but only that it is probable or credible, which in the account of charity, is satisfactory evidence of its truth or reality.

As I would willingly wave needless disputes about words, I shall only say, that if qualifications may be said to be visible, of whose reality we are uncertain, it must be in a less proper sense. Uncertain evidence may discover the possibility, credibility, or probability that a thing exists; but the thing itself, its real existence cannot actually be seen, so is not properly visible, without more light. I grant there may be visible and sufficient evidence of the probability, or credibility of a man's being a saint in heart; and that in the eye or judgment of charity, he is to be reputed, and received as if he were such. And we may say that he is *visibly* such a one to the eye of charity. But in reality, nothing more is or can be seen than external signs or evidences of grace, which are known to be uncertain. The rule and evidence by which charity is to judge, are designed to direct christians how they are to regard and behave towards men in this world; but not to enable them to search and know what is in the hearts of each other.

Whether

Whether then we say that outward holiness forms the character of a visible saint; or that it is the visibility of inward sanctification in the eye of charity which gives one this denomination, it comes to the same thing. For outward holiness is the evidence, the only evidence of grace which the eye of charity can discern. It gives inward sanctification all the visibility it has in the view of the church. Every outward saint is to be reputed a saint in heart, judging of him by the rule of charity, though we doubt not but many such will be found to have been really hypocrites. But the judgment of charity will be further considered hereafter.

There is yet *a third notion of visibility* which requires to be noticed. Visibility is supposed to be the same with the *appearing of a thing to us*, to our apprehension, judgment and esteem. A visible saint is one who seems, and is judged by the church to be a saint in heart. And such only ought to be admitted by them.

But I conceive that, to be a visible saint, is a very different thing, from his seeming, appearing, or being judged, or esteemed by others to be a saint in any sense. It is one thing to say that a thing can be seen by us, and another to say that it is seen, or appears, or seems to us. Visible saintship is a qualification *of the subject*, which *may be* discerned by another. But the appearance one makes in the eye or view of another, is nothing but the *apprehension, judgment* or *opinion* of him who thus judges. A man may be a visible saint, though he may not so appear, or seem, or be judged by the church. And he may seem, and appear, and be judged by them to be a saint when he is no saint in any sense. If the eye or judgment be not faulty or irregular, a visible saint only will seem, appear and be judged to be an external saint, and reputed a saint in heart in the judgment of charity.

But it is the *discernable qualifications* of a person, and not the *discernment* of the church, not the appearance he has in their eye, not the idea, or notion they may have of him, whether right or wrong, which constitutes a visible saint, and gives a right of admission. The reason why one appears, or seems to another to be such a person, may be prejudice, partiality, judging by a wrong rule. But can any think that our right to christian privileges depends on these things? Whoever exhibits, or holds up to view external holiness, or, which is the same thing, credible sufficient evidence according to the gospel that he ought to be charitably reputed and received for a true saint, such a one is a visible saint, and has a right of admission, however he may seem or appear to any. It is not the apprehensions of others, but the qualifications of the proponant, or the sufficient evidences in his favour, duly exhibited which give him a right.

We

We must not then confound the visibility of an object with the sense of the beholder, or with the apprehension or judgment he forms of it. If this be considered, I think it is not true to say *that* to be a visible saint is the same as to appear to be a real saint in the eye that beholds. *That* none ought to be admitted but those who appear, and are judged to be true saints. *That* it is needful that a church have charity for one, or such a favorable notion of him, in order to their receiving him, or having a right or warrant to receive him. It is indeed the duty of the church to judge charitably of all who exhibit external holiness. These have a right to the charity of the church, as well as to be received to communion. But surely, a church having charity for one is not what makes it their duty to receive him. They ought to receive all for whom they ought to have charity (except some accidental bar lie in the way.) And they ought to have charity for all who hold forth sufficient scriptural grounds for it. And external holiness, according to the gospel rule, is such evidence of inward sanctification as gives sufficient grounds for a judgment of charity.

SECTION II.

The Visibility of inward Sanctification, and the Judgment of Charity further opened and stated.

AS it is by means of light that outward objects are visible to the eye, so it is by means of evidence that the mind can discern what is truth, with respect to those objects about which it is occupied. "Whatsoever doth make manifest is light."

Though nothing is *properly* visible but what can be certainly seen, and so really exists; yet such are the relations and connexions which things have among themselves, that we may, from the things which are *immediately* seen, be certain that other things exist; and also that it is *probable*, *credible*, or *possible*, that other things are, or will be, of whose existence yet we cannot be sure. And though we cannot be certain of the *reality* of these, yet the *probability*, *credibility* or *possibility* of them may be known and plainly perceived.

As we have no certain evidence of inward sanctification in another, no more can be discerned than fallible signs, which give us reason to hope, and judge it probable or credible, that such a one is a saint in heart. This is all the visibility which grace has in the eye of charity. And the judgment must keep pace with the evidence on which it is grounded. The one is as doubtful as the other.

Whoever

Whoever exhibits external holiness, exhibits all the evidence of inward sanctification which one man can discern in another. And though this does not make it certain that the subject is a true saint, yet he is certainly a visible saint. And the rule of the gospel, according to which the judgment of charity is formed, requires that every visible saint be reputed, received and loved, as a true disciple of Christ. When a man is admitted into the church as a visible saint, he is admitted as one who gives credible evidence that he is a saint in heart, and is by the rule of charitable judgment to be reputed.

The judgment of charity in favour of any one is not an *absolute judgment* that he is certainly sincere; but only that he exhibits marks or evidences of it. And therefore, according to the gospel rule, is to be so accounted, reputed and received. But it is still understood that the rule and evidence upon which the judgment of charity is formed, leave room for doubt, whether a great part of those who are to be thus reputed, may not be unsound. To repute one a good man, according to the common acceptation of the word, is not the same as absolutely to believe that he is so; but it is to presume that he is, and carry ourselves towards him as if he were such. Every one is to be reputed honest, so long as he behaves visibly in consistency with such a character. And yet when we consider how many who have sustained such a character for a time have forfeited it and become infamous; it would be an irrational credulity absolutely to believe every man to be honest who is of a blameless conversation. So every visible saint is to be reputed a true saint in charitable account. And the judgment of charity is rational, while it proceeds according to the rule and evidence upon which it is to be formed, though we know that this rule and evidence give no certain discovery of the inward character, and spiritual state of men. Nor are we required absolutely to believe further than there is substantial evidence to support us. And there are many of whom we have no reason to doubt but that they are visible saints, and to be reputed and received as true saints, while yet we may have reason to doubt whether they are sincere, and to be jealous over them with a godly jealousy.

It belongs not to the judgment of charity to determine, what degree of evidence external holiness affords of the reality of inward sanctification. We know that it leaves us in uncertainty: It does not exceed probability. But whether it amounts to a preponderant probability, I think cannot be known, unless we could know whether the greater part of visible saints were sincere. If this were supposed, the probability would preponderate in favour of each particular person. There would be more reason to hope

hope he is sincere, than to fear the contrary. But if it were supposed that the greater part of visible saints are not sincere, the probability would preponderate against the several individuals. But though it may be known who are visible saints, yet we know not what proportion of these are sincere. For ought that we know, the greater part of those who give the lowest evidences of sanctification may be saints in heart; and we know not but that the greater part of those who give the best evidences of their sincerity may be hypocrites.

If we cannot know whether one is a visible saint, till we know whether there be a preponderant probability that he is sincere, I think we shall never be able to determine this till the day of judgment.

This, I imagine, will sound like a paradox to some: But let it be examined. I ask then, what external evidences can be depended on as a proof that it is most probable a person is a saint in heart. Let a scriptural rule, with marks, be laid down, by which this may be determined, and it shall be attended to. For my part I know of none. And if the scriptures will not furnish us with rules and marks by which it can be known which way the probability preponderates in this case, much less can experience and observation help us to them. There are some professors indeed who commend themselves much to our charity. But who can say how many of these may be unsound? There are others who appear to us not to adorn their profession as they ought: They have scandalous blemishes in their character. But how many of these may, notwithstanding, be the subjects of sanctifying grace, we shall never know till the day of revelation. If we have no rule by which we can possibly determine whether the evidence in favour of any one amounts to a preponderant probability, how vain must it be to pretend to make this the measure and standard of visible saintship? Or must this be determined by the mere conjectures of christians, undirected by any rule, or by such arbitrary ones as they may form to themselves? This no one will pretend. I conceive then, it is as impossible for us to say, upon any certain grounds, what visible signs of grace make it more probable that any one is a true saint, as it would be to say what outward marks would make this certain. What perplexing doubt must we be in, if we make it a rule to admit none into the church till he exhibits such evidences of sincerity as for the most part fail not? When we know not whether any visible qualifications make it probable, in this sense, that any one is sincere; and can only guess at random, or according to our own fancy; and are never like to know, as long as we live, whether we have guessed right in any one instance.

But

But though we know not whether the greater part of the visible saints are sincere, whether external holiness be a preponderant probable evidence of grace in general, or in any particular instances, yet if we attend to the rule of the gospel we may know who are visible saints, and that they are all to be reputed, received, and loved as the true disciples of Christ. This is the judgment of charity; which without intruding into secret things which belong to God, or indulging precarious conjectures with a rash curiosity, proceeds all along upon safe and sure grounds. We judge according to the rule and evidence though we know that this rule was not given, to enable us exactly to distinguish between true saints and hypocrites, or to determine whether the visible church is chiefly made up of the former or the latter of these characters; or whether the evidence of inward sanctification which arises from external holiness amounts to a preponderating probability.

Some indeed give much greater evidence of sincerity than others; and we may say in a comparative view, that it is more probable that an exemplary professor is sincere than one who does not adorn his profession. But to say absolutely that it is, or is not most probable on the whole that either the one or the other is, or is not sincere, is, I think what we have no rule, or sufficient evidence to warrant us to do.

I might add, that if it were known in general (which it is not) that the greatest part of visible saints are insincere, or if that were supposed, which some have too rashly asserted, that not more than one in ten were saints in heart, and consequently that outward holiness was not so much as a probable evidence, (in the common acceptation of the phrase) yet charity and equity too would oblige us to repute and treat each visible saint as a good man. For surely it would be contrary to all equity as well as charity to judge and treat any individual, as a wicked man, while nothing appears *in him* which would prove him to be of such a character, though it were ever so certain that the greater part were wicked. We may have reason to think that the greater part of mankind is vicious; yet each individual is to be presumed and reputed to be honest, till the contrary appears. If this be thought an unreasonable rule of judging, I would ask whether it would be a better rule not to have charity for a visible saint or admit him to the communion of the church because there are so many hypocrites that the preponderant probability is against each one in particular? Would this favour of charity, or of equity?

In judging of any one by the law of charity we are to judge merely from what appears *in him*, and not from what has appeared *in others*, how many soever, who have destroyed the credit of all evidences in their favour which once appeared in them. Probabilities or presumptions, of an unfavourable aspect towards professions in general are not admitted as evidence against an individual. The visible defection of so many who once were visible saints has induced some to think that much the greater part are not sincere, as has been said; and it may well awaken our fears for ourselves and others, lest after having had a place in the visible church we should have our final portion with hypocrites and unbelievers. But the rule of charity allows us not to think evil of any, or judge unfavourably of them, for the faults of others.

Notwithstanding what has been said, I grant that the evidences of sincerity which some exhibit greatly overbalance whatever *in them* may have an unfavourable aspect. When in judging of the character of a professor, we have, as the rule of charity requires, laid aside all presumptions or probabilities arising from the falling away of so many in the day of temptation, (which might render the integrity of each individual suspected) and estimate his character merely from what is visible *in him*, it may be very plain, that he gives more evidence of sincerity than hypocrisy. And we might say *from what is visible in him*, it appears most probable that he is sincere. And I think none ought to be accounted visible saints *in whom* there are not visibly preponderant grounds of hope. And yet if it could be proved from the scriptures, or from observation, that the greater part of credible professors endure not to the end, but are only temporary believers, this would turn the balance of probability the other way, when the whole evidence was collected and summed up from every quarter.

Indeed, as was said before, I know not but that the greatest part of visible saints may be sincere. What proportion of them is converted we are unable to determine. And I think we had better not pretend to form and give out our conjectures and opinions upon matters of which we are so ignorant, or vainly pry into God's secrets. However, there is no inconsistency in supposing that there may be greater evidences of sincerity than of hypocrisy *in each visible saint*, though it were at the same time supposed that the greater part are hypocrites. For the evidence we may have of the hypocrisy of others, how many soever, appears not *in those* of whom we judge charitably. It is collected from different quarters; and is not the evidence upon which the judgment of charity proceeds.

It may be asked, can there be a visibility without and against probability? Or can that be p[ossi]ble which there is reason to think is more likely not to be tr[ue]? I answer—There must be

more

more than probability, even certainty of the reality of whatever is properly visible. And since we have no certain evidence of the reality of inward sanctification in another, it is commonly held to be an invisible qualification.

But if we take the visibility of sanctifying grace in that improper sense in which only the notion can be admitted, it means no more than such uncertain evidence as the judgment of charity is grounded upon; which makes it not only probable, but certain that the person who exhibits it is to be reputed, received and treated as a disciple of Christ. But whether the greater part of those who hold forth this evidence are disciples indeed, and so whether this visibility amounts to a preponderant probability, we are not able to determine. And if it be thought improper to term that evidence *probable*, which may yet be supposed to fail in most instances; I am not concerned to defend the propriety of using the phrase in this manner; a phrase not found in the scriptures in any sense, but coined in the schools. But this sense, however improper it may seem, is, I conceive, the only sense in which it can be truly said that inward sanctification is visible to the eye of charity by probable signs or evidences; since we know not how often these signs may fail.

But would it not be foolish and contrary to common sense for a prince to admit those into his houshold and armies who he has reason to think may be enemies and traitors? Can it then be rationally supposed that the rule of admission into the church is such, as that more unconverted persons, enemies in heart, may be regularly admitted, than true converts?

I answer. It is certain that the rule of admission is such, that some, yea many unsanctified persons may be, and are regularly admitted. All the congregation of Israel were admitted, or (which is to the same effect) recognized as members of the visible church by God himself at mount Sinai: Yet who can say that one in ten of them were saints in heart? The children of believers are all reputed saints, and as such have a right of admission; yet we are not sure that the greater part of them are inwardly sanctified from the womb, or even afterwards. Nay, it is not doubted but that many, no one knows how many, credible professors, who must be admitted according to the rule, are unconverted. And if this seems to us a foolish rule, which will be likely to operate to the great danger and detriment of the church, by filling it with members inimical to its true interests, let it be remembered however that it is the foolishness of God, which is wiser than men, whose ways and thoughts are high above ours, as the heavens are above the earth.

It is weak indeed to argue against the wisdom and fitness of a rule of admission into the church, because it would be improper to be observed by a prince in forming his army, or family. A prince would not willingly have any who are not really as well as seemingly loyal. But it is the will of God that many be admitted into the church who are not in heart friends to him. And if the greater part be of this character, can we imagine that the true interests of Christ's kingdom are in any danger, while Christ has his enemies as much in his power as any, and can use them as his instruments, or restrain them, or make them his willing people, or cut them off, whenever he pleases?

We may imagine it would be best to have a rule, by which we might be able to distinguish characters so far at least, as to secure a good majority of true saints in every church. And I know not but we have such a rule: Nay I believe we have, if such a rule be best. Some think it would be very desirable, if they could keep all hypocrites out, and admit all true christians; that so church members might have little to do with one another but to enjoy themselves, and keep one another warm and comfortable, undisturbed by perils among false brethren. I doubt not but that Christ could, if he had thought fit, have furnished his churches with such rules, and gifts of discernment, and have so guided and influenced them in their determinations and conduct, that not one hypocrite should be able to creep in. But since he has not done it, we may be certain that the ends he had in view in the institution of visible churches would not be served by stricter and more distinguishing rules than those we have. If we should imagine that we could, from our experiences, observations, and philosophy, spin and weave finer seives than that coarse riddle which the gospel has provided; it would not be lawful for us to regulate our conduct by any rule but that of the gospel. It is not the will of Christ, nor for the interest of his kingdom, that churches be more pure than a due observance of his ordinances will keep them. The house of God needs vessels of wood and earth, as well as of gold and silver. Who knows but that the door of the church is made so wide, that many unconverted persons entering might have access to gospel ordinances, and by them be savingly turned to God? Who knows but that it is the design of Christ, that there should be such in the church as shall furnish frequent occasions for using the ordinances of discipline, that so they may not sink into desuetude? That churches be kept watchful, and shew their zeal in reproving scandalous offences, and their charity in restoring with the spirit of meekness such as are overtaken with a fault. Or if any should remain incorrigible, that others may be

awakened

awakened and warned by such examples to take heed lest they fall? If we wish to screw up the gospel rule a whit straiter than it stands, if we refuse one unconverted person who is regularly ad-admissible, we counterwork Christ's ends; and have reason to expect that we shall be frowned upon, as those seem to have been remarkably who have pretended to form pure churches.

It may also be thought that brotherly love could not rationally be required of, and exercised by Christians towards any but such as give at least preponderant evidence that they are inwardly sanctified. But I ask, How can we possibly divine whether any one has such signs of grace as seldom fail, when we know not what they are, or whether any such signs are visible to us? But the rule of charity is plain and certain. Whoever exhibits external holiness (what that consists in will be afterwards considered) is to be reputed, received and loved as a disciple of Christ for his sake. He has that mark of a disciple, which Christ has appointed as a criterion of those whom he would have us love, and treat as belonging to him. Many of these are not disciples indeed: How many we know not. But in receiving and loving them all we obey his command, and testify our love to his name; which he accepts, as if we had received him. And shall we deem it impossible or unreasonable to have brotherly love for one who has those marks of a disciple of Christ, for which he requires us to have a fervent charity towards such for his sake? Who professes and behaves like a true christian so far as we can discern? Shall we say that such a one is an unfit object of our charity, unless we had higher evidence of his inward state than Christ has thought fit to give us; and knew that the greater part of such are sincere? If any can prove that visible saints are, for the most part, inwardly sanctified, we shall rejoice at the information, it being better than the fears of many.

Upon the whole, since we have a rule by which it may be known who are visible saints, and that all these are the objects of our christian charity; and since we know not whether the greater part of visible saints are inwardly so, and find no rule, by which we can determine certainly who have, or who have not, on the whole, a preponderant probability in their favour; we shall but perplex ourselves in vain, and make the gospel rule useless, if it must first be determined most probable that a person is a saint in heart, before it can be determined that he is a saint outwardly. We may know that the children of believers are visible saints, and are proper subjects of baptism, and are to be received as belonging to Christ. But we should have an insuperable task, if we
must

must first prove it most probable that each one is inwardly sanctified, before we could determine he was a visible saint. We may know that professed christians who are not scandalous are visible saints, and objects of our charity; but how we can know that the greater part of these are sincere, and so that the greater probability is in favour of each professor appears not. If we would take the rule in its simplicity, and acquiesce in the evidence we are to proceed upon, our way would be plain and safe. But when we fancy that the judgment of charity ought to proceed upon higher evidence, and set about refining upon the terms of communion, and straining up the rule so as to comport with our preconceived notions of probability, and satisfactory evidence, and think a majority of true saints in each church is necessary that the interests of Christ's kingdom may be safe, no wonder if we get embarrassed, and our way is so dark that we know not whether we go right or wrong, but can only grope, and guess, and presume.

I have insisted the more on these observations because, if they are just, they are, I think, of importance to be attended to in pursuing the enquiry in which we are engaged, and may help us with more facility and satisfaction to resolve the points which still remain to be discussed.

SECTION III.

That a credible Profession of Christianity constitutes a visible Saint.— What Profession is credible.

THE result of our enquiries, so far as we have proceeded is, *That* visible saints have a right of admission into the church. *That* visible saints may be seen or known to be such, being the subjects of that holiness which may be seen, and which is therefore an external and real qualification. *That* though it is not a certain evidence of inward sanctification, or that the greater part of visible saints are sincere, yet it is the sole, credible and sufficient evidence, upon which, according to the rule of the gospel, the judgment of charity proceeds, in reputing and regarding any as Christians, and gives sanctifying grace all the visibility which it has in the just view of others.

Hence it is obvious to see, that *it is not the reality, but the signs or evidences of grace* which give one a right of admission. Not the certain evidences thereof, or such as are known to amount to a preponderant probability in favour of the whole collective body of visible saints, or of each particular person; but *such evidence as the rules and examples in the New Testament point out or require*. We need not trouble ourselves about the proper signification of the scholastic terms *visible, probable, credible*. All we have to do is to find by what rule and evidence the Apostles conducted themselves in admitting members into the church; and may leave it to others to call it by what name they please.

The point now to be enquired into is, what is visible or external holiness, and wherein does it consist? Or what are those credible evidences of sanctifying grace which give a right of admission?

It has been observed, *that* outward holiness, or (if any chuse rather to call it) the credible evidence of inward sanctification, is a real character or qualification, and not a mere appearance of something whose reality is doubtful. *That* it gives those the denomination of saints in whom it is found. And *that* it comprehends all those signs of grace, which can be exhibited to, or discerned by the church.

But this is not so to be understood, as if one were not a visible saint, unless he should exhibit all the signs of inward sanctification, which the church is capable of discerning. For some visible saints give much more evidence of this than others. Outward holiness appears in very different degrees.

Nothing more is required to constitute an infant a visible saint, and rightful member of the church, than the relative qualification of having a believer for its parent, and so having an interest in the covenant, in which God has promised to be a God to his people and to their seed. For if the root be holy, so are the branches. And if those promises of sanctifying grace, which are made indefinitely to the children of the covenant, that the Lord will circumcise their hearts; that if we believe on Christ we shall be saved and our house, of which their baptism is an outward token; these promises, together with the special external privileges granted to those who are under the outward administration of the covenant, are a foundation for a charitable hope, that infant members are the subjects of sanctifying grace; or however, that in God's own time he will visit them in mercy, and pour out his spirit upon them. They are the subjects of relative federal holiness, being separated and dedicated to God by his covenant. And charity is to presume and hope the best, upon the grounds held forth in the promise which is to us, and to our children. Such an infant is as really a visible saint, and as rightfully a member of the visible church, as the most exemplary adult christian; though much greater degrees of visible saintship may appear in the latter, and charity may have grounds of more confidence

fidence concerning one, whose profession and life expresses purity of heart, than one in whom federal holiness only can be discerned. But it is the reality of visible saintship, in how low a degree soever, which gives a right of admission; though higher degrees carry stronger evidence of inward sanctification. However, the higher degrees are no infallible evidence; and the lowest are a sufficient ground for charity.

But a credible profession of the christian religion is ordinarily necessary to give the denomination of a visible saint, and a right of admission, to an adult person who is not an actual member: Yea, it is by abiding in, and holding fast their profession, that christians maintain the character of visible saints, and a right to continue members, and use the privileges of such. This, I conceive, is the qualification which brings one under the bond of the covenant, and entitles to admission to the privileges of its external administration. To this, external federal holiness is annexed. This is the evidence upon which charity reputes professors to be true disciples of Christ. Nor do I find any thing necessary to give one a right to be admitted as a member of an instituted church, besides a credible profession of assent and consent to the gospel. A conversation answerable to our profession is indeed necessary to maintain the credit of it, after we have taken it upon us. Repentance of former miscarriages, and resolutions of future obedience, are also to be professed as essential branches of christianity. But it appears not that the admission of any professor was held in suspense by the Apostles for one hour, that he might prove the sincerity of his faith by a course of obedience. So that though external holiness, if described in those more eminent and advanced degrees in which it sometimes appears in christians, would include all those expressions of faith, and of the graces and virtues of the christian temper in the life, by which they shine as lights in the world; yet if we consider it in the degree in which it is necessary to constitute an adult visible saint, and qualify for admission into the church, it consists, I think, as was said, merely in a profession of christianity.

If this be admitted, which perhaps will scarce be denied by any, the great point to be attended to is, what is a credible profession of christianity? Or what profession appears to be necessary and sufficient, according to the rule of the gospel, to denominate one a visible saint, to give him a right of admission, and the church a warrant to receive him as a member, and a proper object of christian charity. And our care should be to avoid extremes on each hand; and state the rule so as that it be not too strait, nor too loose.

It will, I think, be granted by all, that it is not sufficient for a man to say, in a general indefinite way, that he professes to be a christian, and to believe that the scriptures are given by God, to instruct mankind in the concerns of religion. There have been some who have called themselves christians, who yet were visibly of a religion as different from that which is plainly taught by Christ and his Apostles, as can well be imagined. It is needless to confirm this by instances. And though we need not judge the spiritual state of those who appear to be grossly and scandalously corrupt in their principles, yet we may judge them unfit for church communion.

Again. A particular and express profession of assent and consent to every article of the christian religion, as contained in the New Testament, is not necessary. Christians in general have not sufficient knowledge to understand the whole system of christianity. There are many points in which they have not yet been instructed, or concerning which they may be in doubt. From the accounts we have of the professions, upon which the Apostles received persons into the church, it would seem that a very brief and general confession of faith might be sufficient. It should however be understood to imply the capital, or most fundamental articles of christianity, faith in Christ, repentance towards God, with resolutions and engagements of obedience to his commandments and ordinances. But, however, I think it appears not from the New Testament that an explicit and formal profession of all the fundamental articles of the christian religion is necessary. We may charitably presume, as the Apostles seems to have done, that men do in a good measure understand and believe such points as are not called in question, but are commonly owned by sober men; and that they will readily receive instruction in other articles, when it shall be proposed to them from the word of God. Now it is doubtless safe to conform to the rules and example of the Apostles.

But a profession of christianity is not credible, if such errors are professed along with it, as utterly and evidently overthrow the truth of the gospel, and render the laws of Christ of none effect; which frustrate the grace of God, or make void his laws.

And there must also be evidence that a professor has a competent understanding of the import of what he professes, and that he speaks in serious earnest, in integrity and veracity, without deceit or designed equivocation. But I think it is not necessary, and ought not to be required as a term of church communion, that any profess, assent to any creed, or consent to any church covenants of human composition, in the terms in which they may be drawn up. Not but that a church has a right to be informed

formed of the religious sentiments and resolutions of those who desire to become members. And our joining with an instituted church purports a confederation, or mutual covenanting to walk together in the order and ordinances of the gospel. Nor is it any ways improper that churches, as well as particular christians, should, as there is occasion, exhibit a confession of their faith, and an account of their order, in such terms as they judge best, to express their understanding of the gospel; but not as making it a term of communion that others profess their faith in the same words. On the contrary, every one should be at liberty to express his christian sentiments as he thinks most proper; nothing more being required than that he speak conformably to the oracles of God. We have neither rule nor example in the New Testament, for churches making any formularies, or canons, expressed in terms different from the words of inspiration, a term of christian communion. And our churches have always disclaimed any such pretence.

Again. A relation of the time and manner in which we have been turned from darkness to light, and from the power of satan to God, is not requisite to our being visible saints, credible professors, and having a right of admission into the church. For to use the words of another, "There is no footstep of any such way of the Apostles, or primitive ministers and christians requiring any such relation, in order to their receiving, and treating others as christian brethren to all intents and purposes; or of their first examining them concerning the particular method and order of their experiences. They required of them a profession of the things wrought, but no account of the manner of working was required of them. Nor is there the least shadow in the scripture of any such custom in the church of God, from Adam to the death of the Apostle John." Thus Mr. Edwards. And I think we might say further, that of all those good men, whose names are recorded in the scriptures, we shall scarce find three instances, of the manner of whose first conversion we have any account. And indeed I know not how it can be known that they ever were conscious of being enemies to God; but might, for any thing we know, be under the influence of sanctifying grace from their earliest remembrance. And how many christians may have been sanctified in like manner from their infancy none can say. And even in those whose conversion to God first commences in adult age, how often is the divine life ingenerated in the manner expressed by our Saviour? " So is the kingdom of God, as if a man should cast seed into the ground, and should sleep and rise night and day, and the seed should spring and grow up he knoweth not how."

how." And as many who could punctually tell the time and manner of their conversion have given great reason to think they never were soundly converted at all, so there are many for whom we are bound to have charity, who will say with that eminent christian, Mr. Baxter, "I know neither the day nor the year when I began to be sincere."

Thus far, I think, christians are generally agreed. But it may be asked further, whether any ought to be considered as credible professors, or admitted as members of an instituted church, but those *who profess saving faith and repentance, and that they consent to the covenant in godly sincerity, and are saints in heart?*

This point needs to be carefully enquired into. Christians seem to have different sentiments upon it. Perhaps they have misunderstood each other, and are not really so wide in their meaning, as some of their expressions would seem to import.

It may be observed, that profession of saving faith, is an ambiguous phrase. It may be taken in two senses. If by it we understand a man's declaring his persuasion that his faith and repentance are saving, this I think is not necessary to give credibility to the christian profession, to render one a visible saint, a proper object of charity.

But if, by a profession of saving faith, we mean such a profession as appears truly to express the religion taught in the gospel, which has the promise of salvation; in this sense it may be admitted that there should be a profession of saving faith. So that if a man's faith or religion be such as his profession properly holds forth, he must be judged to be a true christian who will be saved, how much soever he may doubt, or suspect that his faith, repentance, and religious experiences may be but the effect of common illumination and grace.

First. It is not necessary for a man to profess that his faith is saving, that his repentance and consent to the covenant is in godly sincerity, that he has a confident, or comfortable, or preponderating persuasion of his saving interest in Christ.

Some have thought, a profession of christianity must imply a profession that we are persons of sincere christian piety, true saints in heart: And that none are to be accounted visible saints or disciples, visible members of the christian church, unless they at least pretend to be gracious persons. But this, I think, is a manifest mistake.

For I find *no rule* in the New Testament, requiring professors to declare their certain or satisfactory persuasion that their faith and repentance are saving, or that they are inwardly sanctified, as the necessary qualification for their being admitted as members of an instituted church. I find *no instance or example*, proving or intimating

intimating that a profession of such a persuasion concerning themselves was required of any whom the Apostles admitted, or was exhibited by any upon their joining to the church. Nothing more than a simple profession of repentance, and believing in Christ, and in the word of faith, appears to have been ever required, or offered on any such occasion.

It has been argued, that professing Christ according to the scripture notion, is professing a saving interest in him; and that all visible members of the christian church are those who profess to be gracious persons, as looking on themselves, and seeming, or at least pretending to be such; because *many*, who have had a confident persuasion of their interest in him, and raised expectations of being acknowledged by him, will be rejected by him. But this proves not that *all* members of the church are so confident of their being the subjects of sanctifying grace, and standing in a saving relation to Christ; which is doubtless far from being true. Many true saints, as well as other professors, have not this confidence in their own title to a lot in the kingdom of glory. Much less does this prove, that a *profession* of having such a confident persuasion of our own godliness, and saving interest in Christ, is necessary to our being visible saints, and admissible into the visible church. And indeed who sees not how inconclusive and illogical it is to draw a universal conclusion from a particular proposition? To argue that *all* visible saints must profess a persuasion of a saving interest in Christ, because *many* who have such a persuasion will be disowned by him. *Matth*. vii. 21—23.

Again. If a persuasion that our faith is saving, that we are true saints, and interested in Christ, is not the faith or religion of a christian, by which he hopes to be saved; then a man's professing that his faith is saving, that he is a true saint, interested in Christ, is no profession of the christian faith or religion. Every article of the christian religion is contained in the gospel; and is to be believed upon the testimony of God: And men's professions are to be compared with this rule, and examined by it, that we may judge whether what they profess gives us sufficient grounds of charity. But when men profess that they have saving faith, repent in godly sincerity, are true saints; that they have a confident, or prevailing persuasion of this, they profess something which is not asserted in the scriptures. If our religion be conformable to that which the gospel teaches, it will save us, whatever our persuasion may be concerning our own spiritual state and character. And if what we profess is found to agree with this rule, we must, according to the rule of charity, which presumes that men profess agreeably to their belief, be reputed

and

and received for true christians. But our persuasion, that we are saints in heart, and have saving faith, and interest in Christ, however confident we may be in professing it, is not admissible, according to the rule by which the judgment of charity proceeds, as any evidence in our favour. Our credible declaration of what we think of Christ and the gospel, and not what we think of our own character and state, is the evidence by which it must be determined, whether we are visible saints, and objects of christian charity.

This will further appear, if we consider for what end men are required to profess their religion. It is not to inform the church what one thinks of himself, what opinion he has of his own godliness, or spiritual state: Of this the church is to judge, upon comparing what he professes with the gospel: But it is to inform them what his notions of christianity are, whether he appears rightly to understand it, to approve of it, and receive it as the rule of his faith, the foundation of his hope, and the law of his life. It is not to tell them how well satisfied the professor is that his faith is sound, his repentance and resolutions graciously sincere, and his consent to the covenant cordial; but to exhibit matter of satisfaction to them, that what he professes assent and consent to is the true gospel, as taught in the New Testament. And it is quite impertinent to this purpose, for professors to tell the church of their confident or comfortable persuasion concerning themselves; as if that ought to be of any weight, or as if they had a right to dictate to the church, what their judgment should be.

It may be asked, Does a profession make any thing visible beyond what is professed? What good reason then can we have to judge any one to be a true saint, if he does not profess or pretend that he is one of this character.

I answer—If a man should profess and pretend to be a true saint, all this must go for nothing in the account of the church. His testimony to this is not to be admitted; but what he professes *as his faith* must be tried by the scriptures, whether it be found or not. While he speaks as a *witness*, declaring what his religious sentiments, views and purposes are, the church is to allow him ample and generous credit, if there be no sufficient reason to suspect his veracity. For every man must be allowed to know best his own thoughts, views and purposes. But if he takes upon him the part of a *judge*, or to give his opinion that his faith is found, and will save him, that he is a true christian, a subject of sanctifying grace, this ought to have no weight. He has a right to judge for himself what his spiritual state is; and if he finds reason to judge, or hope that his state is good, he may rejoice in it it. But his declaring this is no evidence to others that he is a proper object of charity. In a word, if what he professes as his religion be found agreeable to the gospel, he is a visible saint; and the rule of charity obliges us to repute him a true saint. But a man's professing a persuasion that he is a true saint, is no part of the evidence on which the judgment of charity is grounded. For we are no where directed in scripture to judge any one to be a saint, because he professes his strong persuasion of it.

When Peter confessed that Jesus was the Christ, he gave evidence that he was born of God, and influenced by the Holy Ghost; though his profession contained no pretence of being regenerated: and whether he had such a persuasion of himself, till he heard the reply which Jesus made, we know not. And whosoever believeth that Jesus is the Christ, viewing his character in the light in which it is displayed in the gospel, is born of God. If then a man's profession gives evidence that he thus believes, it gives evidence that he is regenerated, though he should not profess or pretend to this character. A profession not only makes that visible, or credible, which is professed, but it often manifests other things which are known to be connected with it, and of which the professor might not be aware.

Indeed no good reason can be given why a man's professing a persuasion that he is a true believer, that his piety is sincere, should be thought any great evidence in his favour. Will any say that none ought to be accounted wise and good, unless they would profess and pretend to be such?

Are any more forward and confident in pretending to godliness than many who give least evidence of it? Do any appear more confidently to entertain a good opinion of themselves, or more free to express it, than some of the weakest and vainest of men? Have we more reason to confide in the judgment or sincerity of those who pretend to be persons of piety, and the special favourites of heaven, than of those who pretend to be persons of importance and worth in other respects? In relating matters of fact and experience, of which a man is conscious, and his testimony is called for, we allow him to speak freely concerning himself. In declaring his sentiments, his views and purposes, we admit a credible person as a competent and unexceptionable witness. But if he pretends to give his judgment of his own character, as being wise, virtuous or pious, we may well suspect he is in too much danger of being biassed. He is greatly interested in the case, and little stress is to be laid on his pretences further than they are supported by sufficient evidence. And do we not see that many, who appear diffident and suspicious of themselves, give as good evidence to others that they are sound and sincere believers, as those who profess their own godliness most roundly and confidently?

dently? Muſt theſe be excluded from the number of viſible ſaints, becauſe they ſcruple to profeſs that their faith is ſaving?

There are, it is probable, many ſincere chriſtians who can with all freedom declare what they think of Chriſt and the goſpel, and how they wiſh and intend that their converſation may be ordered, who yet cannot with a good conſcience profeſs that they are ſavingly converted, it being a matter of too much doubt with them. All theſe muſt be ſhut out of the church, if none may be admitted but thoſe who can profeſs gracious ſincerity, and a ſaving intereſt in Chriſt. And though I grant that true chriſtians, if ſcandalous, may juſtly be debarred from communion, yet will any ſay that a chriſtian's ſcrupling to ſay that he is a godly perſon, renders him ſcandalous?

But it may be aſked, Are not exerciſes of grace matter of ſenſible experience? Are not the acts of our will ſubject to our own conſciouſneſs, as well as the acts of our judgment? Why then ſhould not one, who has any grace in exerciſe, be conſcious of it, and be able to profeſs it? I anſwer—It is true we are alike conſcious of the ſenſible actings of our minds, our affections and wills. No one does or can doubt that he has really ſuch apprehenſions, affections, reſolutions and endeavours as he finds and feels in himſelf. The doubt, and danger of miſtake ariſes when we proceed to reflect upon, and examine theſe actings of our minds and hearts, compare them with the rule by which they are to be tried, and then judge of what kind they are. In doing this men are exceedingly liable to deceive themſelves; to take thoſe things for ſigns of grace, or evidences of a graceleſs ſtate, which are not ſo. We are in as much danger of miſjudging as we are of miſunderſtanding the goſpel rule, or of applying it unfairly. If we entertain falſe notions of converſion, and evangelical holineſs, theſe will pervert our judgment of our own character and ſtate. Indeed chriſtians ſee ſo much reaſon to ſuſpect their own judgment of their ſpiritual ſtate, that it is eaſier to give a rational account why many ſhould be ſubject to doubts, than how any can get wholly free from them. If good men may ſuſpect whether they are ſaints in heart, (which none deny) how, can they profeſs that they are ſuch without prevarication, and preſumptuouſly giving teſtimony to what they ſuſpect may not be true?

An eminent divine, who has warmly maintained the neceſſity of a profeſſion of godlineſs as a term of admiſſion to the communion of the viſible church, has yet declared, " That a man's judging himſelf unconverted, and ſaying he did not think himſelf converted, would not hinder him from receiving him who exhibited proper evidence to the church, of his being a convert. That a profeſſion of godlineſs is a profeſſion of the great things in which godlineſs conſiſts, and not a profeſſion of ones own opinion

ion of his good estate." This I think comes fully up to what I have been pleading for: That it is not necessary, in order to a man's being a visible saint, that he profess any degree of confidence that his faith is saving, that he is graciously sincere, and that he has a saving interest in Christ. But how then are we to understand such assertions as these? "All visible saints or christians, all Christ's professing disciples or hearers, that profess him to be their Lord, according the scripture notion of professing Christ, are such as profess (and claim) a saving interest in him, and relation to him:—Look upon themselves now interested in Christ, and the eternal blessings of his kingdom. *All* visible members of the christian church, or kingdom of heaven, are those that *profess* to be gracious persons, as looking on themselves, and seeming, or at least pretending to be such, &c." Can one who says he does not think himself converted, at the same time profess to be a gracious person, to have now a saving interest in Christ, as looking on himself, and seeming, or at least pretending to be such?

This embarrassment, and seeming inconsistency, I suspect, might be occasioned by not distinctly considering, that a man by his profession may give evidence that he is a true christian, savingly interested in Christ, though he does not profess or pretend, or indeed believe that he is such. He may exhibit the premises, but not profess the conclusion which the rule of charity directs the church to draw from them. Peter's profession gave evidence that he was taught of God; yet he professed no such thing concerning himself. A profession of faith is the evidence upon which the church reputes and receives a professor as a true disciple of Christ. And none have a right of admission, but such as exhibit rational and scriptural grounds of charity; not by professing or pretending that their faith is saving, that they are gracious persons, but by speaking conformably to the oracles of God in their profession of christianity.

I am not now considering, whether any who have not a preponderating persuasion that they are true saints can with a right and good conscience make such a profession of religion as may be to the just satisfaction of a church. This case will be examined hereafter. What I plead for is that it is not necessary for a professor to declare his judgment or persuasion concerning his own spiritual state. Such a declaration gives no evidence whether a man's religion be conformable to the gospel, and so is no part of the evidence on which the judgment of charity is grounded.

But *Secondly*. If by a profession of godliness we mean such a profession as gives evidence of christian piety, as being a proper expression

expression of the faith and holiness required in the gospel in order to salvation; this I think should be exhibited in order to admission into an instituted church. There should be a credible profession of assent to the foundation principles of the christian doctrine, of consent to the new covenant; and that without known hypocrisy or reserve. In a word, *a profession expressive of the faith, temper, and resolutions of a true christian*, as described in the gospel. If this be what is meant by those who require a profession of godliness, or saving faith as a term of christian communion; this is no more that what Mr. Stoddard has also declared as his stedfast persuasion.

Such a professor is a true christian, if his profession be a true and proper representation of his mind and heart. And could we be sure of his veracity, and that we rightly understood his meaning, and also the true meaning of the gospel, we might by comparing these together, know that they did agree, and consequently that his faith would save him. But we cannot be certain of these things. We know not whether a professor aims to give us a true account of himself: But charity requires us to presume that he does so, unless we have evidence of prevarication. Suppose we have no reason to suspect his *veracity*, yet what he means to profess may be different from the sense in which we understand his words. But we are to judge a professor's meaning to be conformable to his words fairly and candidly interpreted. If his expressions are consonant to the words of the gospel, we presume that his meaning is also agreeable to the sense, the truth, and spirit of the gospel, unless we have evidence of the contrary. Finally, If a man's professed sentiments should agree with our own, it may still be doubted how far our own are right. For the church is not infallable. But they can judge no otherwise of any profession, than by comparing it with what they conceive to be the true meaning of the gospel.

So that the judgment of charity proceeds upon favourable presumptions, which are known to be uncertain: So uncertain that, as has been said, we are not sure whether the greater part of those for whom we ought to have charity are sincere. But if one whose profession appears to us sound and unexceptionable, discovers neither hypocrisy nor misunderstanding therein, we have all the evidence in his favour that is ordinarily to be expected from a profession. And it would be uncharitable not to receive and regard, and behave towards him as a true christian.

A sound profession of christianity may be termed a profession of saving faith; not because the professor says that his faith is saving, but because what he professes appears to express the truth and spirit of the gospel, which is effectual to the salvation of all

who

who receive it. But no profession which can be delivered in words is a certain discovery of the true sentiments and dispositions of the heart. For words are but the artificial and arbitrary signs of those ideas which they represent or express; and so are capable of being used and understood in as many different senses as men may put upon them. No honest man indeed will designedly equivocate in professing his faith before the church, or seek to deceive them with ambiguous expressions. But whoever speaks, however sincerely, uses words in his own sense: and they who hear will understand his words in their own sense; perhaps diverse from what was meant, and perhaps the sense of both may differ from the proper evangelical sense in which the Apostles spake. Hence arises manifold ambiguity in language, so that it is impossible for any one to profess his faith but in words which are capable of being used and understood in different senses. For instance—If one should profess to believe in Jesus Christ as the Son of God, and Saviour of mankind; it is not easy, to reckon up all the different ways in which this proposition has probably been understood; the different notions men have had of the person and character of Christ, the character of God, in what sense Jesus is Christ, and Son of God, and Saviour of men; and finally what is the import of believing in him. Whoever believes in Christ in the proper or evangelical sense has saving faith. But the object of faith with many professors is not the true Christ, or the true God whom the Apostles preached to the world, nor do they in a proper gospel sense believe on him.

Since then the language of mortals is and will be ambiguous as long as they annex different ideas to the same words, and consequently whoever professes christianity must do it in language subject to this great imperfection and inconvenience; a question will arise—How is a church to understand the professions which are exhibited from time to time? Are they to take them in a good and favourable sense, when the words will fairly admit such an interpretation, and no reason appears for unfavourable surmises; or are they to take them in some supposeable sense contrary to the truth and spirit of the gospel? Now the rule of charity is, whoever professes his faith in words which when candidly interpreted agree with the scriptures, is presumed to mean the same for substance which the inspired writers did, and consequently that his faith is sound and will save him.

There is then no just foundation for the odious reproach which has been cast upon some, for saying that professions of faith are to be taken in a favourable sense, though delivered in terms capable of being otherwise understood; as if they meant to encourage designed equivocation This certainly is not taking words in a favourable or equitable sense. If any think they can help mankind to a language not ambiguous, or can effectually remedy this great imperfection, that so men may no more misunderstand each other, they will by doing this perhaps put an end to almost all disputes among christians, and remove a main difficulty in the forming of pure churches.

But as this is not expected at present, we must, if we profess our faith at all, do it in words which may be understood variously. And when our profession fairly holds forth a good sense, and is consonant to the form of sound words delivered in the gospel, it would be injurious as well as uncharitable, for any to presume, without positive evidence, that our intended meaning is unsound and corrupt. Every sound professor, is in the charitable account of the church, a true believer, unless there be positive proof of the contrary. And the best sense which words will bear, when fairly and candidly interpreted, must be presumed to be the true intended meaning.

SECTION IV.

Of Professing in Moral Sincerity.

THE dispute which has been warmly agitated—Whether it be a profession of godliness or a profession of the christian religion in moral sincerity which gives a right of admission to external communion has risen, as it seems to me, chiefly, if not wholly from misunderstanding.

For they who maintain that a profession of godliness is necessary, declare also that they do not hold it necessary for a man to say, or even believe that he is godly. But those are to be admitted who exhibit proper evidence of this, that is, such evidence as may be a foundation for a judgment of rational charity.

On the other hand, they who hold that a profession of christianity in moral sincerity gives a right of admission, declare withal that they mean "such a profession as shall make it visible or credible to a judgment of rational charity that men are savingly converted, circumcised in heart ; and that none are to be admitted, who do not make a public and personal profession of their faith and repentance to the just satisfaction of the church ; none but such as are, in a judgment of rational charity, believers ; and carry themselves so that there is reason to look upon them to be saints."*

A profession

* Stoddard.

A profession of christianity in moral sincerity, as it is explained by those who make it the term of communion, seems to come to the same effect with a profession of godliness, as that is explained by those who plead for the necessity of it. Both agree that there should be such a profession as shall make it visible, or credible to a judgment of charity, that the professor is a true christian; and that this is sufficient.

It will be said, that professing christianity in moral sincerity is not a proper and credible evidence of grace, in a judgment of rational charity. Let us then examine this matter a little; and see whether a fair and candid explanation may not serve to take away this *apple of strife*, which has occasioned hard thoughts and trouble to so many. And I hope the friends of peace and charity will not disapprove the attempt.

Some have declared themselves at a loss to understand what moral sincerity is. It has seemed to them a phrase without any intelligible determinate meaning. I know not what dark vague notions some may have had. What I understand by it is *moral truth*; that is, *veracity*, aiming to express one's real sentiments; in opposition to wilful lying, deceit, prevarication, and misrepresentation. When a professor aims to give an honest and true account or expression of his religious views, and purposes, he is morally sincere, however erroneous his sentiments may be, or however improperly expressed. An infidel or heretic, as well as a sound believer is morally sincere, if he does not knowingly and designedly misrepresent his own thoughts; even though he should express himself so improperly, that others should take his meaning to be different from what he really intended. The phrase is also, though more rarely, applied to other acts besides profession. So a man may be said to repent in moral sincerity, when he is really sorry for his vicious practices, and resolves to do so no more; though perhaps his repentance may not be evangelically sincere, not flowing from gospel principles and motives. So when one consents to the covenant sincerely, as far as he knows himself, and understands the nature and tenor of its proposals, he consents in moral sincerity; that is, unconscious of hypocrisy; however he may mistake in his views, and his heart not be perfect before God. But should one profess to own the covenant, while he found no heart to consent to what he understands it to import, he would be morally insincere, and convicted in his own conscience of hypocrisy.

Gracious sincerity, I conceive, is a real conformity of soul in its views and temper to the truth and spirit of the gospel; or a good and honest heart from the influence of gospel principles and sanctifying grace.

Whoever

Whoever professes christianity in moral sincerity professes to assent and consent to it really and heartily, so far as he understands it, and knows himself, whatever doubts he may have whether he have that spiritual discernment which is the effect of saving illumination, and whether his heart may not deceive him. Let us now examine whether we may and ought to have charity for such a professor: to repute and receive him as one who is hopefully a true christian.

In the first place—It is supposed that we have credible evidence of his being morally sincere in the account he gives of himself and his religion. That he means not to deceive us. That he does not knowingly and wilfully prevaricate, disguise, or misrepresent his sentiments. Charity obliges us to think thus of every one who seriously pretends to speak in veracity, and gives us no sufficient reason to disbelieve or suspect it.

Secondly. It is supposed that he professes assent and consent to the gospel, as he understands it, and so far as he is conscious of the actings of his own mind and heart. And surely if we can have confidence in his veracity, that he aims not to deceive us, he must be allowed to be a competent and unexceptionable witness of this—Whether he believes christianity to be the true religion, and, as far as he understands it, approves of, and consents to it, and resolves to regulate his mind, heart and life, conformably to this rule.—For this is matter of conscious experience. He speaks of what he knows, and testifies of what he sees and finds in himself. But how shall we be satisfied whether he rightly understands the gospel? Whether what he professes may not be a false notion, a perverted gospel; and not that truth which the Apostles believed and taught? That we may be able to judge of this,

Thirdly. He declares, at least in some capital and fundamental articles, how he understands the doctrine and precepts of christianity which he professes. And if the account he gives of his religious sentiments, dispositions and purposes, when fairly and candidly interpreted and compared with the gospel revalation, appear to be unexceptionable, expressing the truth and spirit of christianity. Then,

Fourthly. Upon the testimony of the gospel itself we may believe, that he whose sentiments, dispositions and endeavours are conformable to the doctrines and precepts of the gospel, is a saint in heart, born of God, and shall be saved. I ask now, If a man shall in moral sincerity, or veracity, exhibit a profession of his faith, repentance, and consent to the covenant, which, when examined by the gospel, shall be found to harmonize with it, and properly express the faith, the spirit, the desires, and resolutions of a true christian,

christian, is this no sufficient ground of charity? or rather what better ground can any profession give?

Two things are necessary to give credibility to any ones testimony or profession; *That* he means not to deceive us; and *That* he is not deceived himself. We may be as well satisfied that a man means not to deceive us, as we are that he is morally sincere. And we have as much evidence that he is not deceived, as we have that the intended meaning of his profession is agreeable to the gospel.

When a man professes to be morally sincere, he gives testimony to a fact in which he can scarce be deceived. Since no one can wilfully prevaricate without being conscious of it upon the first reflection. But when he professes to be graciously sincere, this is a fact in which men are in great danger of being deceived: And whatever confidence we may have of their veracity, their judgment may often justly be suspected. And the scriptures inform us not what is the spiritual state of any particular professor. Is then a man's professed persuasion that he is graciously sincere and savingly interested in Christ, a better and more rational ground of charity, than if he, without pretending to give his own judgment concerning his spiritual state, should, with professions and marks of veracity or moral sincerity, express the sentiments, temper, and resolutions of a christian as exhibited in the gospel? Nay, Is there not a much better ground of charity in the latter case than in the former?

It is not merely a profession of moral sincerity which makes one a visible christian. No one, I presume, ever meant, or said so. Nay a profession of infidelity, or antichristian principles, if morally sincere, would evidence a man to be no christian. It is a *profession of christianity*, which recommends to the charity of the church. If this be exhibited in moral sincerity, we conclude that it is agreeable to the sentiments of the professor: If it be also agreeable to the gospel, we conclude that it is sound and good. And consequently that the professor is a sound believer, and good christian. And we know that all such are graciously sincere, and will be saved.*

It is true a man may profess and seem to be morally sincere, when he is not so. And however sincere, he may express himself improperly; which may occasion misunderstanding and error in the judgment of the church concerning his faith. His expressions

---

* Mr. Stoddard held that a profession of faith and repentance in moral sincerity is a credible evidence of saving grace.—" Such a profession" says he, " as being sincere makes a man a real saint, being morally sincere makes him a visible saint."—Grace makes one a real saint, credible evidence of grace, a visible saint.

sions may be unexceptionable, when his intended meaning is unsound. And therefore, as was said before, no profession a man can make will certainly manifest him to be a real christian. Nor is this necessary in order to his being evidently a proper object of christian charity, a visible saint, qualified for admission into an instituted church.

Obj. 1. It may be objected that *saving faith* is the condition of an interest in the covenant, and a title to the seals thereof; and a profession of this is requisite as a condition of admission to them.

Answ. It is not grace, but evidences of grace, not certain but credible evidences which constitute a visible saint, and give a right of admission. A profession of the christian religion, with credible marks of moral sincerity, is evidence of something more and better than moral sincerity; even that a man is a true christian. It is the condition or qualification to which a right of admission is annexed. The covenant proposes not only terms of salvation, but terms of external church communion. Inward sanctification is the condition of the former; visible saintship of the latter. Credible professors are visible saints. They who profess christianity in moral sincerity, are credible professors. "It is a miserable mistake," says Mr. Shepard, "to think that inward real holiness is the only ground of admission to church membership, as some Anabaptists dispute: But it is federal holiness, whether externally professed as in grown persons, or graciously promised to their seed."*

Obj. 2. Moral sincerity is a transient vanishing quality, and so is no fit qualification for a standing privilege. I answer—

Since it is not the reality but evidence of grace which gives a right of admission, I would ask, what evidence can be exhibited by profession, which can more be confided in as unfailing? Do not those who profess to be saints in heart often fall away? A profession of christianity, in moral sincerity, for what yet appears, is as likely not to fail, as any profession which can be made. When any fall away from the christian profession, or destroy the credit of it, they forfeit the privileges of christian communion. The privilege is as vanishing as the qualification for it.

Whoever is qualified for admission is *fit* for it. Visible saints are qualified. Credible professors are visible saints. A profession of christianity in moral sincerity is credible, as has been said. This gives that fitness of which we now speak; and which the rule of admission requires—If any who were regularly admitted become unfit to continue members, this proves not that they were

---

* Church Membership of Children, page 13.

were unfit when they were admitted. It is uncharitable for us to judge a credible professor to be unconverted. But if we should so judge of any one; yea, if an angel from heaven should declare that he was unconverted, yet if he made an unexceptionable profession of christianity, and were not scandalous, I see not how he could be refused without transgressing the rule of the gospel. It is not our *believing* a professor to be sincere, which makes it our duty to receive him, but it is the conformity of his profession to the gospel, not discredited by a scandalous life. Christ who knew the hearts of men, admitted some into the number of his disciples who were not true believers on him. He was no unwise builder, nor did he put unfit materials into his church. But he received those who exhibited the qualifications required by his own rule, though he knew that many of them would not continue in his word.

Indeed a standing in the visible church is a privilege of no long duration to any. And it is in vain to think of forming an instituted church of durable materials. We shall all be soon cut off from the visible church by death, if we should not be cast out of it before. And while we remain in it, may fitly enough be compared to "*blocks of ice*" in a building, daily melting away. And this waste is no otherwise repaired than by a successive accession of new members, who will in the course of nature soon fade and fall off like "*leaves*." The instituted church is but as a tent provided for our accommodation, while we sojourn in this wilderness. It is the invisible church alone to which christians have a permanent union. In this house of the Lord they are built up as lively stones, and will dwell therein forever.

Obj. 3. If a profession of moral sincerity give a right of admission, the greatest part of church members are like to be such professors as are not even morally sincere. Since moral sincerity without grace, commonly soon fails and is lost. I answer—

It is not sincerity of any kind which gives a right of admission, but credible, though uncertain evidence of it. It is not evidence of moral sincerity merely and abstractly considered, which give a right of admission, but as connected with, and giving credibility to a sound profession of christianity. If those who give evidence of sincerity are secretly hypocrites, this is no bar to their being received. When they manifest hypocrisy they are to be rejected. This rule duly observed, the church will never consist chiefly of professors visibly insincere: Nay, not one visible hypocrite will be admitted to, or suffered to continue in external communion. But we have no rule for excluding concealed hypocrites, how many soever. And it is contrary to the law of charity to judge them to be such.

Obj. 4. A man may profess christianity in moral sincerity while living in heinous wickedness. I answer— It

It is not the heinousness of men's sins, which makes them unfit to be admitted; but it is their being scandalous. Credible professors, not scandalous, have a right of admission, however heinous their wickedness may be supposed. Scandalous persons are to be rejected, not because they are judged to be graceless; (we need not judge their state) but because they are visibly unfit for communion.

I have briefly touched these objections, so far as the rule and right of admission might seem to be affected by them; though I am sensible that the principal aim of those who urge them, is to prove that moral sincerity in professing christianity, does not give any one a lawful right to *come into* and have *active communion* with an instituted church in the use of special ordinances; but that godly sincerity is a necessary qualification for this. We shall therefore have occasion to consider these things further, when we come to consider, who have a right of access to the special privileges of rightful church members.

The issue and result of our enquiries may be summarily delivered in the *rule* following, viz.

All who give evidence of a competent understanding of the fundamental articles of the christian religion, and with credible marks of veracity, or moral sincerity, profess their assent and consent to them, not overthrowing the credibility of their profession by scandalous errors or practices joined with it, are visible saints, and to be reputed true christians in a judgment of charity, and to be loved and treated as such: And upon their request, and consenting to a covenant of confederation, are to be admitted as members of an instituted church, together with their children, and to all such privileges of communion as they appear actually capable of, and meet for.

SECTION V.

The Right of Admission to full Communion considered—Who are the Subjects of it.

AFTER what has been discoursed of the right of admission into the church as members, it will be no long or difficult task to define and state in a general way, who have a right to be admitted to the special privileges of members in full communion.

This distinction of members into those who are confirmed, perfect, in full communion, or complete standing, and those who are not so, is generally acknowledged in all churches, except those of the Anabaptists: And it appears to have been received from the earliest ages of the church. This is not to be understood as if any who belonged to the church were but *half members*, or not really, completely, and perfectly such; but that some by reason of their unfitness and incapacity to have active communion with the church in some ordinances, or to use them to the glory of God, and their own spiritual comfort and benefit, are not at present to be admitted to them. Though all rightful members have a *right* of *heirship* to all the external privileges of an instituted church, yet as heirs in minority, they are not admitted to possess and use all privileges at their discretion, till they appear to be actually meet for, and capable of it in some competent measure.

The special external privileges of members in full communion are chiefly these two—A right to partake at the Lord's supper, and to give their votes with the church in such matters as come under their cognizance. The latter is in our churches limited to the brotherhood, agreeable to an apostolic canon, which suffers not a woman to speak, or give her voice in the church, or to usurp authority over the man, but to be in subjection. But members of either sex are admitted alike to the Lord's supper.

A right of admission to the privileges of a member in full communion belongs only to those who exhibit some measure of *actual fitness* to attend and improve those special ordinances and privileges in such a manner, as that the ends of their institution may be answered in them.

They should manifest so much spiritual knowledge, such establishment in their holy faith, such dispositions of piety, as may give reason to hope that they will adorn their profession by an exemplary life. It should also appear that they so far understand the nature, the ends, and proper uses of the Lord's supper, as to be capable of examining themselves, and discerning the Lord's body, and so eating that bread, and drinking that cup in remembrance of him, as that their souls may be nourished by the bread of life, and their spiritual edification subserved and promoted. Not that high attainments in christian knowledge and piety need to be exhibited to give one a right of admission: but such only as may manifest a capacity, and disposition, in the use of such helps and advantages as are enjoyed in the church, to use special ordinances to the glory of God, the honour of the christian profession, and the spiritual benefit of the communicant. And perhaps there are few adult professors qualified for admission as members, might not also be regularly and properly admitted to full communion.

CHAP.

CHAP. V.

Of the RIGHT of ACCESS to the PRIVILEGES of EXTERNAL COMMUNION.

SECTION I.

The Right of Access explained and distinguished; founded not in the Reality but Evidence of Grace in the view of Conscience.—Assurance, certain Evidence, prevailing Persuasion, preponderating Probability of Grace not necessary.

A RIGHT of coming into an instituted church, of joining to it as a rightful member, of having active external communion with it in a joint use of special ordinances and privileges, I shall, for brevity of expression, call—*A right of access.*

This implies a right in the proponant, to do all that is necessary to be done on his part, in order to his becoming a member, and using the privileges of one: That is, to propose himself as a candidate, and ask admission; to make such a profession of christianity as may be to the just satisfaction of the church, that he is a proper object of christian charity, and ought to be received as such; to take upon himself the bond of the covenant, and attend upon those ordinances which belong only to rightful members.

The question then is, who have this right of access, as above explained; a question which perhaps may be thought more difficult to be resolved upon certain and safe grounds, than that concerning the right of admission. And it is well known that christians have been divided in their judgment upon it; and the consciences of many have been burdened with scruples, of which they never could be fully eased. For however plain it may be that a professor may and ought to be admitted, yet if his right of access be not good and valid, he is not a rightful member, but has intruded without warrant, and must answer for his presumption.

It is plain that the case before us is quite distinct from that which we have been considering; and is to be resolved upon different grounds and principles.

The qualifications to which the right of admission is annexed are visible to the church, viz. external holiness, a profession of faith. But the qualifications which give a right of access are seated in the inward parts of a man, his mind and heart, and cannot be seen by others. Therefore,

It belongs to the church to judge who have a right of admission: But they cannot, and pretend not to determine who have a right of access. This case is judged in a different court, even that of a man's own conscience. Each one must judge and determine this for himself.

Again. The right of access differs from that of admission in its immediate object. The right of admission is *a right to have a privilege granted* to the subject. The right of access is *a right to do certain actions*. The former might be called for distinction a *passive right*, or *title*, the latter, an *active right*, or *warrant*.

Further. They differ remarkably in their foundations. The right of admission is founded in the covenant grant of special privileges to such as have the qualifications specified. But *the right of access is founded in, or arises from a sufficient reason in the view of the subject*. Whatever any one sees a good reason for doing, he has a right to do. This, and this only, gives a sufficient *warrant*.

No one can act morally without some reason. Nothing can be a reason to any one till he has a view or apprehension of it: Nor has he a right to act upon any reason or motive unless it appear to him good and sufficient, and be *rightly* judged to be so. If we judge the reasons prompting us to do an action, to be sufficient when they are not, our unreasonable judgment gives us no right to act according to it. It is an unfaithful guide, and ought to be corrected. It must be *the dictate of a right conscience*, discerning and approving the reasons for doing any thing, to give us a right or warrant to do it.

But it is to be remembered, that when we judge according to our rule, and the evidence we are to proceed upon, our judgment is morally and practically right, though the facts judged of should be really otherwise, than we take them to be. The evidence upon which we are to form our judgment in many cases is not infallible, and so leaves us uncertain what is the real truth of the fact. But our judgment is certainly right and reasonable, if it be conformable to rule and evidence, whether it be conformable or not to the truth and reality of the thing. The practical judgment, or the dictate of the conscience what we may or ought to do, may be right and sure, when the speculative judgment is doubtful or mistaken. Thus, there are many who doubt whether they are fit for the privileges of external communion with an instituted church, or entitled to them by a covenant grant; and yet the reasons persuading them to ask for admission, and attend the administration of special ordinances, may be such as their consciences, when rightly informed, must judge sufficient to warrant their coming. Their *title* to the privilege may be doubtful to the speculative judgment, because supported only by probable evidence. But their *warrant* to come and take, and use the privilege may be certain and evident to the practical judgment; because *probable* evidence is *certainly* a sufficient reason for us to determine our conduct by in numberless cases, and in this in particular. If they have so much evidence of their title as amounts to a sufficient reason for them to act upon, this is enough to put it out of doubt, that their conduct may and ought to be determined by it: That is, they have a *right* or *warrant* to act accordingly.

This then we lay down as a principle, or maxim. No one has a right or warrant to come into the church, who has not sufficient reason for doing so, in the view of his own mind; and whoever has such a reason has undoubtedly a warrant to come, whatever doubts he may have respecting his spiritual state, and whatever his state may be supposed to be. A good reason in view, is a good foundation, and the only foundation for the dictate of a right conscience that we have a warrant to do any thing. It is vain to imagine any deeper or more substantial foundation necessary. It is *evidence alone* which gives a right to act, for this only can furnish the mind with a good reason for its conduct. Inevident realities no more affect our warrant in this case than if they had no existence.

Hence it appears that inward sanctification, while inevident, gives no right of access. He who knows not that he is a true saint may have a *covenant title* to the invisible grace and blessings of the gospel. But while this is secret to him it can be no *reason* in his mind, no *warrant* for coming to ordinances. If grace was that qualification which of itself gave a right of access, then all true saints would have a warrant to come at all times. But this is not true. Their warrant must be evident to them. It is not valid, and may not be acted upon, till it is acknowledged and signed in the court of conscience. It is not lawful for us to do any thing without the approbation of the judge in our own breast. An inevident warrant is a nullity: It gives no right to do any thing: It is not the supposed reality of inevident qualifications, but it is the evidence we discern of our title to privileges which gives us a *right*, a *reason*, a *warrant* to ask for and improve them.

It may be said, though it is not grace, but the evidence of it, which immediately determines the judgment or dictate of the conscience, and so furnishes us with a reason or warrant for coming into the church, yet grace itself is a necessary qualification, that

that our right or warrant for coming may have a proper and solid foundation. That is, it is necessary as a foundation for that evidence of grace, and that judgment or dictate of our own conscience, to which our right of access is annexed. I answer—

It is granted, that a man must have evidence in his own mind of inward sanctification, in order to his having a right to join himself to a church. I mean sufficient evidence to be a good reason for his doing so. And I grant also, that if none but true saints have such evidence as to furnish them with a sufficient reason for coming, then sanctifying grace is necessary as a solid foundation for a right of access. But if some who are not true saints may have such evidence of sanctification, as may furnish them with a sufficient reason for coming, then inward sanctification is not necessary as a foundation for a right of access. But whether any, except true saints, have good reason to ask for, or use the privileges of church members, is a question we shall let rest for the present. We may be able to judge better of this, when we have considered who have a good reason for joining themselves to a church, and using special ordinances: and what evidence of inward sanctification a man must have in his own mind, that he may have a reasonable inducement to do so. To proceed then—

When the point to be determined is, whether I may or ought to come into the church, and use the privileges of a member, or not, the better and weightier reason for either alternative is sufficient to determine the practical judgment, though it may leave room for the speculative judgment to doubt of my spiritual state. In speculation, a stronger probable reason does not make it *certain* that *that is true*, which is supported by it. For what appears probable sometimes is found not to be true. But even in speculation the stronger reason ought to turn the scale of assent against a weaker, though it can only beget a doubting opinion. But in practice, the stronger and better reason is a sufficient ground for a sure dictate of conscience, determining what I may and ought to do. For it is certainly my duty and right to act agreeably to the best light that I have, and determine my conduct by a stronger reason, rather than by a weaker presumption to the contrary. If I have credible, though uncertain evidence that I am *entitled*, according to the gospel rule, to the privilege of being a member of a church, I have a weightier reason for coming and using this privilege, than I have for neglecting to do so. And I am sure that it is not only my right but duty to determine my conduct according to the weightier and better reason; so that in this case the conscience or practical judgment may *certainly* determine that I have a *right or warrant* to come accordingly. We
often

often have occasion to form a judgment upon uncertain evidence: And if we judge fairly, and according to the rule and evidence, our judgment is right, though it should not be conformable to the real nature of things. And the dictate of conscience respecting our conduct in this case is right and *sure*, notwithstanding doubts or mistakes of the speculative judgment arising from the want of more certain evidence. Our right and warrant to act or conduct ourselves, in many cases, arises from reasons in our own minds grounded on evidence of facts which we know to be uncertain. But our rights and duties grounded on this uncertain evidence are sacred and sure.

Whoever therefore, upon a fair judgment of the case, according to the gospel rule, finds stronger and better reasons to think it his right and duty to become a member of an instituted church and attend its special ordinances, has a right to come, yea, is bound to do so; notwithstanding any doubts he may have whether his qualifications be such as give him a *covenant title* to these privileges. If he has reason to think it *probable* that these privileges are granted to him, and that he is commanded to take and use them, he may be *certain* that he has stronger reasons to seek access to them than to neglect them; that it is his *duty* to determine his conduct by these stronger reasons rather than by a weaker presumption to the contrary: And that he has *a right to do* what is most reasonable to be done in the case supposed.

Though it is granted that none have sufficient reasons and warrants for coming into the church in the judgment of conscience when rightly informed but they who find *credible marks or evidences* of sanctifying grace. Yet I would not be understood to assert that it is necessary for a man to be assured, or confidently or prevailingly persuaded of his being inwardly sanctified. It is one think to discern credible signs and evidences of grace, and another to be persuaded we are really the subjects of it. As there are many who cannot but be conscious of black marks of hypocrisy upon them, who yet will confidently presume their state is good, upon mistaken principles; so there may be many who also upon mistaken principles, draw sad conclusions against themselves, notwithstanding they are conscious of such signs of sincerity as *might reasonably* encourage comfortable hopes. They find not but that they heartily believe the christian religion, and desire to have their hearts and lives conformed to it, and yet judge themselves to be unconverted, because not conscious that they have been turned from a state of sin and impenitency in such a way, and such a sensible order in their experiences, as they suppose is necessary to a sound conversion. Perhaps they have never been fully convinced of being in a state of impenitency, enemies to God, dead in trespasses and sins; which they are told is an evidence that they are still in a state of unrenewed nature: not considering that they who are under the influence of sanctifying grace from their earliest remembrance, never find themselves in a state of nature, and cannot be truly convinced that they are enemies to God. But it would be endless to reckon up the doubts and scruples with which many christians are troubled, thro' the darkness and mistakes of their own minds, the workings of sin and vanity within them, the power of temptations, and the weakness of their faith and graces; whereby they may be hindered from *crediting* or taking the comfort of those evidences of sanctification they find in themselves. Therefore it is not a man's being persuaded whether more or less confidently of his being a true saint which gives him a right of access, but it is his finding in himself hopeful signs of christian piety. What these signs are in particular we must learn from the scriptures. And this enquiry shall be attended to presently. But whoever finds these in himself has a warrant to join himself to the church; whatever his prevailing judgment may be concerning his spiritual state.

It is acknowledged by all that some *ought* to come into the church, and so have a *right*, a *good reason* to do so, who have not an undoubting persuasion, or certain evidence in their consciences that they are saints in heart. If this were necessary, no doubting christian, none but they who have attained to the assurance of hope ought to come. But this none will say. Certain evidences of sanctification are not necessary by the consent of all. Nor can it be said that such evidences are necessary as have a real and certain connection with a state of grace, though it may not be necessary that the subject know this connection. For the right of access is not grounded on any thing secret and unknown to him by whom it is exercised, but upon known and sufficient reasons and evidence in the view of a right conscience. But an unknown connection of evidences with a state of grace can be no reason for any one to act upon. It can add no strength or validity to his right or warrant.

Nor do I think it necessary that a man find such evidences of sanctifying grace as are known to make it *more probable*, and so produce a *prevailing persuasion* that he is a true saint. If my judging it to be most probable that I am a true saint be necessary to warrant my coming into the church, then it is also necessary that I have a rule, and proper evidence to ground this judgment upon. Otherwise it will be only a random conjecture or presumption. But I find no rule, no marks by which one whose sincerity is doubtful can determine upon sure grounds whether or no it be on the whole most probable. There are rules by which we

may

may try ourselves whether we are true christians. And if comparing ourselves with these we are in doubt, there are other less certain marks, which, if we find in ourselves, we may hope comfortably, though we have not assurance. That is, If we are not conscious of hypocrisy in religion. But how do we know whether the greater part of those whose hearts condemn them not of hypocrisy, are sincere christians ? How can a doubting christian determine whether the hopeful but uncertain signs of grace which he finds in himself (for to him they appear uncertain so long as he is doubtful) whether these be oftner than not connected with the reality of inward sanctification? Whether the greater part of such dubious characters as his own appears to himself, may not be those whose hearts are not right with God? And consequently whether the probability preponderates in favour of himself, or any one in particular ?

A profession of christianity is credible evidence to the church that the professor is a christian, though it is not known whether the greater part of professors be such. And if I am not conscious of hypocrisy, this is a credible evidence in my own conscience that I am sincere. But as I know not whether the greatest part are sincere christians, who are unconscious of hypocrisy, how can I know whether this amounts to a preponderant probability ?

We have reason to think that some, we know not how many, are insincere in the profession and practice of religion who are not conscious of it. And therefore though my heart reproaches me not, yet I cannot say that this makes it most probable on the whole that I am a sincere christian. And yet if, after careful examination of myself by the word of God, I find hopeful marks of sincerity, not invalidated by evidence of hypocrisy, I find more reason *in myself* for comfortable hope, than self condemnation. This I call *credible evidence of sanctification in the view and account of conscience.* And this I think all who come into church communion ought to have. But to make it a rule, *that none may come but those who judge on sufficient grounds that it is on the whole most probable they are true saints* must leave the consciences of all doubting christians in inextricable perplexity.*

SECTION

---

* If it were known that the greater part of the money of a particular stamp and date were counterfeit, it would then be more probable that each untried piece in particular was counterfeit. If it were only known in general that much of it was counterfeit, but whether the greater part or not was uncertain, we should then be unable to determine whether any untried piece were most probably counterfeit or not. But if it were enquired concerning any such piece whether any special signs of its being counterfeit appeared *in it*, we might then say, if no such signs appeared in it, that it had a fair appearance of being good. But yet as perhaps the greater part of what looked as well, was not good, we could not say whether it were most probable that this particular piece were good.

SECTION II.

What Evidences of Sanctification give a Right of Access to Special Ordinances.

IT has been observed that a right of access is a right or warrant to act. That this arises from a good reason in the view of the agent. That it is not grace, but evidence of grace, which furnishes a man with a good reason for coming. That certain evidence is not necessary. Nor such evidence as is known to amount to a preponderating probability: But that lower evidence is sufficiently credible to satisfy a right conscience that it is more reasonable and safe to come than to refrain: And that it is certainly our *duty* and *right* to act the more reasonable part in all cases. We are now to enquire what are those credible evidences of sanctification which render it warrantable for one to come into communion, with an instituted church.

As visible saintship exhibited to the church in a credible profession of christianity gives a right of admission, so visible saintship in the view of conscience, or a consciousness of assent and consent to the christian religion, so far as we understand it, and know our own hearts, gives a right of access. Indeed, if we speak properly, whatsoever is visible is real and certain. But it is not such a visibility of inward sanctification as begets assurance, which is required in this case. For though the assurance of hope be attainable, yet none will say it is necessary to our having a right of access. But they who have credible, though uncertain evidence of sanctifying grace, may warrantably come.

And as those who *give evidence* of moral sincerity or veracity in professing christianity have a right of admission, so they who *are conscious* that they can so profess, their hearts not condemning them of hypocrisy, may warrantably profess accordingly, and ask admission. But they who cannot profess in moral sincerity, as before explained, have no right or warrant to profess christianity, and so must be barred from rightful communion with the church. For known falshood and prevarication in professing religion is impious presumption.

Hence it appears, that all who know themselves to be unconverted have no right of access. Such are not visible saints in the view of their own conscience. They find not credible evidence of sanctifying grace, but know themselves to be graceless. They cannot profess christianity in moral sincerity; but must be conscious

scious that they do not heartily assent and consent to it. For though moral sincerity, in the profession and practice of the christian religion, is not a certain evidence of inward sanctification, yet it is such a credible positive evidence of it, that whoever finds it in himself cannot know himself to be unconverted, unless by supernatural revelation. It would be inconsistent to suppose that one who knows himself to be an unbeliever, and disobedient in heart and life to the gospel, should at the same time be conscious that he does really believe and consent to it without reserve, so far as he knows himself. He who is conscious of this has reason to hope, though he may not be certain that he is sincere. He may suspect himself notwithstanding, and even think it more probable that his heart is not perfect before God. This has probably often been the case of true christians. But how one who can profess in moral sincerity should know himself to be insincere, is to me as inconceivable, as for one to know that he speaks falsly, when he is aiming to speak truly.

I conceive then, that all those may warrantably and rightfully come into church communion who are visible saints in the view of their own conscience, as before explained. That is, all who find that, so far as they understand the gospel, and know their own minds and hearts, they do believe, approve and consent to it without reserve, and are willing to give up themselves to God in Christ according to the terms of the new covenant, resolving without delay to forsake every known sin, and persevere in the practice of every known duty. These have such hopeful evidence of christian piety in themselves, that they have reason to think it is their right and duty to join themselves to an instituted church.

If the church is bound to judge one to be a visible saint, and receive him as one who exhibits credible evidence of true piety, when he makes a sound, intelligent and honest profession of christianity, so far as they can judge, and is not scandalous in his life: then he who finds not but that he does sincerely believe, approve and consent to the gospel, so far as he understands it, and is not conscious of indulging himself in known wickedness, such a one (whatever he may think of his state, and whatever it may be supposed to be) is a visible saint in the eye of his own conscience. He has credible evidence of grace in himself, whether he have the truth of it or not; and may as reasonably have charity for himself, (if the expression may be allowed) and come for the privileges of a rightful church member, as the church may have charity for him, and admit him.

Some may perhaps think it too slender evidence in favour of a professor, that he is morally sincere; that his heart condemns him not of insincerity in the profession and practice of christianity. I

L

grant

grant it is not a certain evidence of grace, nor is this neceffary to give a right of accefs, as all allow. But it is not a contemptible ground of hope. If our hearts condemn us not, then have we confidence towards God. Many who profefs godly fincerity, have really no more certain evidence of it than this, that they are not confcious of hypocrify in profeffing and practifing chriftianity. They who have this evidence in their favour, however they may fufpect themfelves, have reafon to hope they are fincere. But they have a good reafon, warrant, right to take upon them the chriftian profeffion, if they can do it without known hypocrify.

For will any fay a man cannot have reafonable fatisfaction that he is warranted to confefs Chrift before men, join with his profeffed difciples, and declare himfelf on their fide, by worfhiping with them in the ufe of gofpel ordinances, till his faith has been proved to be genuine? Is there any rule or example in the New Teftament from which fuch a conclufion can be gathered? I think not.

The Apoftles received thofe into the church without delay who profeffed to believe that Jefus was the Chrift the Son of God, the Saviour and Lord of men. It appears not that they waited to have their faith proved by works or trials, either to the church or to their own confciences. A bare profeffion of faith fatisfied the Apoftles that they were fit to be admitted. And the conviction the hearers had of the truth of the Apoftles' doctrine fatisfied them of their right and duty to profefs this belief, and join with others who protefted the fame. What confidence they had that their faith was of fuch a kind as would not fail, but be found upon trial, to praife, honour and glory, appears not; nor whether any of them were fully perfuaded of their own godly fincerity before they joined to the church. After they were admitted, they were exhorted to make their calling and election fure, and attain to the affurance of hope, by their diligence in works and labours of love, and in the duties of their heavenly calling. The Apoftles taught that it is by keeping Chrift's commandments we know that we know him. And they exhort thofe to examine themfelves whether they were in the faith, whofe right of memberfhip they did not call in queftion.

As there is no gofpel rule requiring a church not to admit a profeffor, unlefs they were fure, or perfuaded that he is a true faint, (though indeed they ought charitably to repute every credible profeffor to be fincere) fo there is no rule forbidding a hearer to come into the church, unlefs he be well perfuaded that he is a true faint. Nor can this, I think, be argued from any thing in the New Teftament. We find not that Chrift or the Apoftles refufed any who defired to profefs their faith, and join themfelves

to

to the disciples, though he knew, and they were doubtless apprehensive that many were not disciples indeed. Nor do we find that they ever cautioned them not to presume to come, till they had good satisfaction touching their spiritual state; or that they reproved any as rash and too forward in offering themselves before they had sufficient evidence that their conversion was sound and saving. This seems very remarkable, when it is considered how suddenly, and in what numbers they flocked into the church, sometimes thousands in a day.

It may be thought that these primitive professors were assured, or at least persuaded, that they were in a state of favour with God: "For upon their embracing the gospel, they were filled with joy and praised God. That the account of them now is not as of persons under awakening, pricked in their heart, weary and heavy laden sinners, but of persons whose sorrow was turned into joy, looking on themselves as now in a good estate." I answer—Since they had professed their faith to the satisfaction of the Apostles, and were admitted to baptism by them, this must be matter of much comfort and joy to them, though they might still have doubts whether their hearts were sincere. Besides, we need not imagine that their joy and praises arose only, or chiefly from a persuasion and sense of being the favourites of God, and in a good estate. Is not the gospel glad tidings of great joy to those who are pained with a sense of sin, guilt and the wrath of God? Must it not rejoice such, before they are satisfied whether their sins are forgiven, to hear and believe *that* there is forgiveness with God: *That* he delights in mercy: *That* Christ came into the world to save sinners, and there is salvation in him: *That* hope is set before them, to which they may fly for refuge, and escape the wrath to come, and be the happy subjects of that grace which bringeth salvation? I might further ask, Would it not fill a benevolent heart with joy to know that many have been, and will be saved from sin and misery, and blessed with all spiritual blessings in Christ? And is it no matter of joy and praise to a christian to behold the glory of God's grace as displayed in the gospel? We need not imagine that those primitive christians were so selfish as not to be able to find any thing in the gospel to excite their joy and praises, till they were first satisfied that themselves were objects of divine favour, and in a safe and happy state.

To proceed. They who most insist that sanctifying grace is necessary to qualify for a rightful access to special ordinances, yet grant that they who upon examination, find reason to hope they are sincere, are bound in conscience to come, though they may have many doubts. And that they who find that they truly believe

lieve and consent to the gospel, so far as they know themselves, have reason to hope they are sincere.

Now, they who are morally sincere in professing christianity, have all this evidence that they are real christians: For moral sincerity is opposed to conscious hypocrisy. If such have not a warrant to come, how can any come with a good conscience, who doubt their own sincerity and spiritual state?

Will any deny that one, who after serious examination of himself, is uncertain whether he be a true saint, may yet be certain that he finds hopeful evidence of sincerity in himself? Or, that one who is not conscious of hypocrisy in the profession and practice of the christian religion, finds more reason *in himself* to hope he is sincere, than to think he is a hypocrite, however he may see cause to suspect himself, from the inclinations to sin he finds in himself, from the falling away of so many eminent professors, and other grounds of fear which he sees in himself and others.

Now, may not such a person, notwithstanding his doubts, have reason to think, yea to have an *undoubting persuasion*, that the inducements and encouragements he has to join himself to a christian church are greater, than any discouragements arising from the scruple before mentioned? May we not safely determine that he whose conscience bears him witness that he can sincerely, so far as he knows himself, profess all that is required to be professed by those who are admitted to communion, has unquestionably more and better reason to come forward, and give honor to Christ and his gospel by such a profession, than to retrain till he has certain evidence that he is a true saint, or at least is sure that this is on the whole most probable; which I think no doubting christian, will ever be able to determine? And if, as I conceive, such a person may have clear and undoubted evidence and conviction in his own conscience that the reasons persuading him that he may and ought to offer himself for admission are of more weight than the scruples which tend to discourage him, I would ask, Is it not evidently most reasonable, that a weightier and better reason should determine his conduct, rather than a weaker doubt or scruple on the other hand? And if this be granted, which I think all must grant, I would ask again, Is it not undoubtedly the right and duty of such a man, and of every man, to act rationally; and practically to prefer a stronger and better reason to a weaker one to the contrary? Whether the better reason, in this case, does not lay a sacred obligation upon a man to determine his conduct according to it? Whether it ought not to weigh down what is evidently of less weight? and though it may leave the speculative judgment in doubt as to his spiritual state, yet it directs the conscience *rightly and certainly to determine* what we reasonably

may

may and ought to do in such a doubtful case? That is, *to determine certainly and rightly*, what is our duty and right to do. In a word, Is not a manifest preponderancy of *reason* and *evidence*, on one side of the question, *a sufficient warrant* for us to act upon? If so, then they who have *more and weightier reason* for coming into church communion than refraining have a good warrant and lawful right to do so. If not, then none have a sufficient reason, or are allowed to come, but those who have full assurance of their own good estate. For, as was argued before, not inevident qualifications, however real, but evident and sufficient reasons in the view of our minds give us our right and warrant to act in all cases.

Since then inevident sanctification is no reason or warrant to act upon, and so can give no right of access to special ordinances; since it is sufficient reason and evidence in the view of the mind which gives this right; since certain evidence of inward sanctification is not necessary, but credible though fallible evidence is sufficient by the consent of all; since the practice of the Apostles in admitting professors into the church, without waiting to have them prove the truth of their faith to the church, and to their own conscience shews that, this proof is not necessary to give one a right of admission and access, we must conclude that as a sound profession of the christian religion exhibited apparently in veracity or moral sincerity makes a man a visible saint in the account of the church, and gives him a right of admission; so conscious veracity or moral sincerity in assenting and consenting to the christian religion, makes him a visible saint in the view of conscience, and gives him a warrant or right of access.

It may be said, that if one judges his spiritual state to be better than it is, he deceives himself; which he has no right to do; and his error gives him no right to privileges. I answer, If he proceeds according to the rule and evidence by which he ought to judge in the case, he has judged rightly and regularly, whether he has judged truly or not. Nor is it contrary to truth for one to judge that he has those marks of sanctification of which he is conscious, though he cannot conclude positively, from uncertain credibility or probability what his state is. But a positive conclusion that our state is good appears not to be necessary in this case.

SECTION

SECTION III.

Doubting Christians may have a sure Warrant or Right of Access.

FROM the preceeding discourse it appears that a man who doubts whether the command of Christ requiring his disciples to attend the special ordinances of the gospel speaks directly to any but to true christians, and whether any but such have a covenant grant of, or title to them, and also whether himself be a sincere christian, may notwithstanding these speculative doubts, be sure that it is his duty and his right to come into church communion. For whether a command be directly addressed to us or no, yet if we have plainly more reason to judge that it speaks to us, this is sufficient to bind us in duty to yield obedience to it. And whether we are *really entitled* by a covenant grant to a privilege or not, yet if we have credible evidence that we are rightful subjects, this gives us *a warrant, a lawful and certain right*, to make use of it. *Uncertain titles give certain warrants till they are found to be null and void.* We are often uncertain whether the title by which we hold our property be valid. Whether the relations mankind are presumed to stand in one to another are really such as we take them to be. Indeed we seem to be for the most part in a degree uncertain with respect to the real existence of those facts and circumstances, on the supposition of which our rights and duties are founded. Yet our rights and duties are certain and unquestionable, so long as we have credible evidence of the truth of these circumstances and facts.

We may also from what has been argued above see that whoever comes to special ordinances must have *a known or evident right* in order to his doing it, with a good conscience. If by a right we mean what I call *a passive right* or *a covenant title* to ordinances in the outward administration and inward efficacy of them, then I conceive that one who *is not certain*, nor fully persuaded of this may not only have a *right* to them, but also a *warrant* a *sufficient reason* to come to, and attend upon the outward administration of them. For whoever has *credible evidence* in his own mind, that these ordinances are by the gospel covenant granted to and enjoined upon him, is bound in duty and has a good reason and warrant for coming to them, notwithstanding he may not be *certain* whether he has a *covenant title.*

But if by a right to ordinances we mean, *what I call an active right.* That is, *a good warrant, a sufficient reason* for coming to, and attending upon them, then no one may or can with a good conscience

conscience come till he is satisfied beyond doubt that it is more reasonable for him to come than not, and consequently that he has *a warrant to come*. Casuists, agree that it is unlawful for a man to do that, the lawfulness of doing which he doubts. This rule is grounded on the words of the Apostle in Rom. xiv. Let every man be fully persuaded in his own mind. To him who esteemeth any thing unclean to him it is unclean. He that doubteth is condemned if he eateth, because he eateth not of faith; for whatsoever is not of faith is sin. This is not to be understood as if the Apostle declared it to be unlawful for one to act upon probable evidences and reasons, which might leave the speculative judgment in doubt as to the truth of facts. For it is often our duty to act upon very uncertain and slender presumptions. But we are not allowed to *do* that which we doubt whether it be lawful, and reasonable, and warrantable for us to do when all things are considered. We must have a reason in the view of our minds for acting as we do: And this reason must be evidently better, and of more weight than any reasons we have to the contrary. And if the reasons for doing any thing evidently preponderate, they give an evident or known warrant or right to do it in the judgment of reason and a right conscience. Till this appears a right conscience cannot sign the warrant. And without the leave or consent of our own conscience, we are not allowed and have no right to do any thing.

Object. 1. But it may be objected that it is unreasonable to say that a man may not take any privilege 'till he knows he has a right to take it. For then we must do nothing upon a probable judgment and hope. We must neither move, nor voluntarily forbear to move, without a certainty of our duty in the case one way or other. There are many doubtful cases, in which a man must act according to the best of his judgment. If he judges according to the best light he can obtain that it is his right and duty to come into church communion, he may be bound in conscience to do so, notwithstanding he may doubt of his right, and by doing otherwise he would act unreasonably, and run himself into what he thinks the greater danger.

I answer.—If it be unreasonable to say that a man may not take any privilege till he knows he has a right to take it, then the contradictory position is reasonable. That a man *may* take a privilege when he knows not that he has a right to take it. That is, he *may do it lawfully*. In plain words. He has an evident right to do what he has no known right to do. Which is, I think, a contradiction. If we are often obliged to act upon doubtful evidence (as it is certain we are) then we have a right to act on doubtful evidence. For necessity gives us a right, nay obliges us to do what must be done. And if it be evidently reasonable in such cases to act according to our best judgment, and to be determined by those reasons, and that evidence which is of most weight; then we have a right, and ought thus to act and be determined. So that the evidence of our right to do any thing is inseparably connected, and keeps pace with the evidence we have that it is necessary and reasonable for us to do it. And if no one may come to ordinances while he doubts whether it be *most reasonable*, for him to come, then he may not come while he doubts whether it be his *right* to come.

And here it again falls in our way to observe, that it is not sanctifying grace which gives a right or warrant to come into church communion. For since none may come but those who are *fully persuaded* that it is most reasonable, and consequently their duty and right to come, which implies a full persuasion, that they are possessed of that which gives them this their warrant; and since some who *are not fully persuaded* that they are the subjects of sanctifying grace have confessedly a right of access; it follows that such have more certainty of their right of access, than of their being true saints, which could not be, if it be supposed that sanctifying grace gave them their whole right.

Object. 2. If no one may come to ordinances while he doubts whether it be his right or duty to come. An unconverted man may not come, if he has any doubt of the right of the unconverted. I answer.

If it were supposed that the unconverted might have a right of access to special ordinances, it is easy to see that such may be sure of their own right, without knowing whether the unconverted have a right to the same privilege. If any one finds that he can profess the christian religion without known hypocrisy, and consequently that he has preponderating reasons and encouragements to use the ordinances, he may be sure it is his duty and right to come to them. But though this is sufficient to ascertain to him his own right and warrant, it must still leave him in doubt whether any unconverted have the same right unless he could know whether any such had as sufficient reasons for coming as he finds in himself. But as he knows not that he is unconverted, his own warrant, however certain, will not enable him to conclude positively and certainly that any unconverted have a like warrant; though he must in reason conclude, that if any such have credible evidence in their own conscience that they are sincere christians, and that it is most reasonable for them to seek admission to the privileges of the church, then it is their right and duty to do so. For every one may and ought to do what is most reasonable, as has been said. But no one who is fully persuaded that *sincere christians*

christians only have a right or warrant to communicate with the church in special ordinances, can warrantably come to them or attend upon them in faith and a good conscience, while he doubts his own sincerity. He may not come, unless he is on good grounds *persuaded beyond all doubt that he is a sincere christian.*

Obj. 3. If all who come to ordinances must have an undoubting persuasion of their right or warrant to come, the unconverted are effectually barred by this rule. For since they have not an undoubting persuasion of the truth of the gospel, and so know not whether the charter be authentic in which alone the right of any to christian privileges is conveyed, they cannot have an undoubting persuasion of their own right. I answer—

That no unsanctified person is fully persuaded of the truth of the gospel, is more than I have ever seen proved. If the devils have a full conviction of this, I see not why unsanctified men should be thought incapable of it. But not to insist upon this—I say, It is a great mistake to imagine that the scriptures lay no certain obligations, and convey no certain rights to those who are not assured of the truth and divine authority of them. For if it appears probable, or credible that the gospel is a divine revelation, this is enough to fasten sacred and important obligations on the conscience; obligations as certain and unquestionable as any which can arise from the most assured conviction of its truth. If the gospel is believed to be *most probably* a divine revelation, then it is *most certainly* the duty and right of all who are thus persuaded seriously to observe its rules and precepts.

If I judge it probable that the gospel is divine, and if I find that it calls upon all to attend to its proposals upon their peril, am I not undoubtedly bound in duty to hear the word? And have I not a certain, unquestionable, known right to do so? Are any duties and warrants more certain and unquestionable than many which are grounded only on moral and probable evidence? Can I not *be certain* that I have a right to use a privilege which the law of my country gives me, unless I have not only moral, but infallible evidence that my title is good, and the law valid.

We have no more than moral and probable evidence of the authenticity of human laws, or constitutions; but is it therefore *uncertain* whether it be our duty or right to obey them, or take the benefit of their protection? *Is it uncertain* whether a man has a right to claim or receive a legacy bequeathed to him, because wills are proveable only by moral and fallible evidence? *Is it not certain* that a credible, presumptive title, nay, mere profession of a privilege *bona fide* gives a right to make use of it, in such ways as are not injurious to others. In short, if it be probable that a law is authentic, the subject who thinks so, is certainly bound to obey

obey it. If I have reason to think it most probable that I have a title to any privilege, I have reason to be certain that I have a right to take and use it, till the contrary shall appear, especially when this is a matter of duty as well as right.

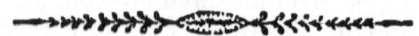

CHAP. VI.

Of the RIGHT of the UNCONVERTED to EXTERNAL COMMUNION.

SECTION I.

Reasons in favour of the Affirmative.

BY the foregoing rules and maxims, we may now modestly examine that much disputed question, whether an unconverted man may have a right to be a member of an instituted church, and use the privileges of a member in full communion. If then such a one may be a visible saint, having and holding forth credible evidence of inward sanctification: If such a one may be able to profess the christian religion without known hypocrisy, heartily assenting and consenting to it, so far as he understands it, and knows his own mind and heart. If such a one may have stronger reasons to think it is his right and duty to come than to refrain: That the duties and privileges of a member in full communion belong to him. If such a one may have and exhibit credible evidence of a measure of actual fitness for communion with a church in special ordinances; and if there be no known bar in the way of his coming, and being admitted; must we not conclude, that he has a right to be admitted, and is bound and has a warrant to come.

I presume none will deny that such a one has a right to be admitted as a visible saint in the just account of the church. A credible profession of christianity, with evidence of a measure of actual fitness for special ordinances will entitle to this. And none will say that all such credible professors are converted. All the doubt is, whether one who is unconverted may have a right, a warrant, a sufficient reason, a weightier inducement to come than to refrain:

For

For I have before shewn, that these several phrases amount to the same thing.

To bring the question then to its proper statement, let it be observed, that it is not enquired whether those who know themselves to be unconverted, or who find no heart or freedom to assent to the doctrines, and consent or submit to the laws of Christ, have a right to profess, in known hypocrisy, and so join themselves to the church, and come to its ordinances. This would doubtless be presumption.

Further. The question is not whether those may come who can find no positive evidence in themselves that they believe the gospel, and consent to the covenant of grace therein proposed. Without this no one is warranted to make a profession of christianity. These are all excluded by the rules above laid down.

So that the question will come to this, whether any can have the warrants and encouragements to come into church communion, which have been shewn to be sufficient, and ought to have more weight to determine the conduct than any scruples and discouragements to the contrary, and yet be unconverted. Let us review the particulars.

Will any deny that an unconverted man may be morally sincere in professing christianity? Is it a certain mark of inward sanctification for one to find that, so far as he knows himself, and understands the gospel, he holds it for true, approves of it, and resolves to make it the rule of his faith and practice? Is it not possible, nay credible that some who are not conscious of hypocrisy may not be upright in the sight of God?

Will any say that no unconverted man, upon examining himself can find credible reasons to hope, that he does rightly understand, assent to, approve the gospel, and resolve without delay or reserve to seek salvation in the way there revealed? Or is every one converted who can find any credible, though uncertain evidence of these things in himself? May not a man have some grounds of hope, who has not certain evidence of his good estate? Is no evidence of faith credible but such as is found only in true believers, and so is infallible? And is it not supposeable that such marks of saving conversion as are not infallible, however they may give reason of hope, may be found in some who are not savingly converted?

May not an unconverted man be a visible saint in the just account of his own conscience, as well as of the church? And is he not so, if he finds in himself hopeful evidences of being a true christian, the holding forth of which entitles him to admission to external communion?

May not an unconverted man be interested in the covenant in respect of its outward administration? Is not this the case of all
the

the unconverted children of church members as long as they live, unless they are cut off according to the rule of the gospel, for known covenant breaking, impenitently persisted in? Want of inward sanctification, while it is not evident, nor scandalous, does not, according to the gospel rule, uncovenant one, or disqualify him for continuing a rightful member. Have not rightful church members a right to come, and be admitted to the outward ordinances; which are granted by covenant not to the invisible church, as such, but to visible instituted churches? Ought any one to be debarred or refrain from coming, if neither he nor the church *has evidence* that he is unqualified? And is it not credible that some such may notwithstanding be unconverted?

Is it unlawful for those to have communion with an instituted church in the use of outward ordinances, who are not prohibited by the gospel from coming, or being admitted? Are any interdicted in the gospel but such as *evidently* want the requisite qualifications? And may not some be unconverted who *appear not* to be unqualified for external communion?

Have not those a warrant to use special ordinances who have reason to think it is their right and duty so to do? Have not those reason thus to think, who have credible evidence that they are interested in the covenant, qualified to come and be admitted to ordinances? And may not some unconverted have credible and hopeful signs and evidence of this? Or will any say that certain evidences of grace are necessary to give one a warrant to act in this case? Or, that uncertain signs never fail, that is, are infallible?

Should any think that no unconverted man has credible evidence that he is sincere, or qualified in any measure for the duties or privileges of external communion, or has a right or warrant to come to them, that no such person has good reason to think he ought rather to come than refrain; he must at the same time hold, that no one has a warrant to come unless he has certain and infallible evidence of sanctification. For those marks and evidences which are found only in true saints, and not in any unconverted man, are certain and infallible. Upon this supposition, every one may be as sure of his being a true saint, as that he finds any grounds for a comfortable hope. But will any say this?

I shall only add, that if doubtful evidences of sanctification may furnish one with a good warrant to come into church communion, it being more reasonable and safe for such a one to come than refrain, as all seem to allow; and if there may be such doubtful credible signs of grace, and fitness for the duties and privileges of external communion in some who are unconverted; which cannot be denied, unless we say that doubtful evidence is

certain

certain and infallible; I see not but that we must conclude, that some who are unconverted may have a right or warrant to come, as well as be admitted to external communion, which was to be proved.

SECTION II.

Objections considered.

OBJECTION 1. If grace be not necessary to give a right to special ordinances, why are none allowed to come or be admitted but those who have and exhibit evidence of grace? If moral sincerity be sufficient, why should any thing more be professed or manifested?

Answer. It is the evidence, and not the reality of grace which gives a professor a right or warrant to come, and the church a warrant to receive him. Wherever this evidence appears, this right is annexed to it: Whether there be a foundation for it in the reality of the thing intimated by it, or not. It is granted by all, that probable evidence is a reasonable and sufficient warrant to act upon in this case: That is, it gives a right to act: And yet we know that what is probable sometimes has no real existence. But the rights and duties founded upon probabilities are as real, as certain, and as important as any. Whoever has and gives evidence of moral sincerity in professing christianity, has and gives evidence of saving grace. For moral sincerity, in such a profession, is itself a credible evidence, as has been shewn.

Object. 2. If some have a right of access to ordinances in the fight of God who are unconverted, and yet the church may not admit them, unless in their sight and judgment they are true saints; then the eye of man must require higher terms than the eye of God.

Answ. They who have a right to ordinances according to the rule of the gospel, have a right in the sight of God. Visible saints, according to the rule of the gospel, have a right to the ordinances. Credible professors are visible saints in the view of the church, and have a right of admission. Professors, whose hearts condemn them not of hypocrisy, are visible saints in the view of conscience, and have a right of access. The eye of man looks for, or requires no higher terms than the eye of God; but the very same, that is, *visible saintship.* Charity *hopes* that visible saints are sincere, but knows it is uncertain whether they are so or no. That *rational evidence* of gospel holiness which gives a right of admission;

admiſſion; and that *charitable belief*, which the church is to have of the faintſhip of thoſe whom they receive to communion, leaves it ſtill a matter of uncertainty in the eye of the church's chriſtian judgment, whether they are ſaints indeed. Nor has God made it neceſſary for us to believe that men are truly pious in order to its being our duty to admit them. We are allowed, nay required to admit credible profeſſors, be our opinion of them what it may. If we are uncharitable, that is our fault, which will not juſtify our refuſing thoſe who hold forth credible evidence of chriſtian piety. It is the *evidence* exhibited, and not *the judgment or opinion* we may form of profeſſors, which God has made neceſſary in order to our lawfully admitting them to communion.

It is not therefore true that the church is required and allowed to admit none, but ſuch as are truly pious in their ſight, or whom they judge to be ſuch. For they are allowed and required to admit *all whom they have reaſon to account* truly pious, in a judgment of charity, whether they are ſuch in *their* ſight and judgment or not. And they have reaſon thus to judge of all credible profeſſors, though they know it to be uncertain whether they are truly pious. Again, It is not true that churches are forbidden to admit any, unleſs they firſt have evidence obliging them to *believe it certain* that they have goſpel holineſs. We know that all the evidence we ordinarily can have in the caſe muſt leave us uncertain of this. It can in reaſon only oblige us to believe *that it is credible or probable they are ſaints*, though poſſibly they may be but hypocrites. Now, If ſome for whom the church ought to have charity, and who are in their eye true ſaints, ſo far as their eye can diſcern, may yet be unconverted, and if theſe according to the rule of the goſpel ought to be admitted to communion, then ſanctifying grace is not neceſſary, though credible evidence of it is neceſſary to give a right of admiſſion. Again—If they who can profeſs the chriſtian religion unconſcious of hypocriſy, and who know nothing of themſelves which would prove that they are inſincere, have reaſon *comfortably to hope* that they are the ſubjects of ſanctifying grace, and *certainly to conclude* that they are viſible ſaints in the eye of conſcience, and if ſuch have reaſon to think it is their duty and right to come into church communion, as has been argued; and if it be ſuppoſeable that ſome of this character may not be true ſaints, then ſanctifying grace is not neceſſary, though credible evidence of grace is neceſſary to give a right of acceſs.

Object. 3. None have truly a right to take and uſe any covenant privilege but thoſe who are really in the covenant: none are in the covenant, who do not comply with, or poſſeſs the condition or terms of it; and this none do but true believers. For ſaving faith, or a cordial conſent to the terms of the goſpel, is the condition

tion of a covenant interest and right. But unconverted sinners do not consent to the covenant, but reject it, and so have no right to any of its benefits.

Answer. It is not true that none have a right to take and use any covenant privilege but those who are in the covenant. All gospel ordinances are covenant privileges. Yet those who are not in covenant have a lawful right to attend to the dispensation of the word, to have and search the scriptures, whenever providence puts them into their hands, and to join with the church in assembling and worshipping God. It is granted, however, that none but those who are in covenant have *a covenant right* to these privileges, and that there are some privileges to which none but those who are in covenant can have a *regular access*. Of this kind are those institutions called special ordinances, which are granted, and appropriated to the church. But then,

It is not true that none are in the covenant but those who have complied with the conditions of the covenant. For the children of church members are confessedly in covenant, and of the church, before they are capable of complying with any terms or conditions ; unless we call their being born of church members a compliance with the condition, though it be no act of the children ; yet the covenant grants a baptism right, with other special church privileges to such children, though numbers of them are unconverted. So that unconverted persons may really, rightfully, and in the sight of God be interested in the covenant, so as to be regular members of an instituted church, and intitled to special privileges pertaining to the outward administration of the covenant : And according to the rule of the gospel they must continue such as long as they live, unless they *appear* to be unfit and unworthy.

Therefore—It is not true that saving faith, or a cordial consent to the covenant, is the condition of an interest in it, as outwardly administered, and of a right to outward church privileges. It is indeed the invisible condition of a right, to invisible privileges and blessings dispensed immediately by Christ. But a right of admission to outward privileges is annexed to conditions or qualifications discernable by men ; viz. a credible profession of christianity. And it is the right and duty of those who can and do profess christianity unconscious of insincerity to ask for and use these privileges. Though we are not certain that such a professor is a saint inwardly, or intitled to the invisible blessings of the covenant, yet we may be certain that he is a saint outwardly, and may come and be admitted to the outward privileges of an instituted church.

Object. 4. The unconverted are forbidden to own the covenant. " To the wicked God saith what hast thou to do that thou shouldest

shouldest declare my statutes, or take my covenant into thy mouth?"

Answer.—I grant it would be unlawful for those professedly to covenant with God, who had at the same time convincing evidence that their professions were but hypocrisy, which appears to have been the character pointed at in the text. They who are *evidently* wicked, would but enhance their guilt by owning the covenant, and attending ordinances hypocritically for a pretence. But we never find men reproved for entering into covenant, when they did it sincerely, so far as they knew themselves. By the wicked we are here to understand those who *appear to be so*, by such black marks of impenitency as we find in the following context. But these words were never meant, to discourage those who seriously and without known hypocrisy, desire to own the covenant, and walk in the commandments and ordinances of the Lord; but those only who are forward to make a public profession, while allowing themselves in known wickedness. In short, as *evident qualifications* alone give a right to ordinances, so they only who are *evidently wicked* are here forbidden and debarred from coming to them.

It is most certain that none are allowed to make a lying profession. But this is not done by those who profess in moral sincerity. For how any one can lie in veracity I understand not. If men fulfil not their covenant engagements they are no doubt highly blameable. But this proves not that it was unlawful for them to come under these bonds. If we may not form good resolutions till we know we shall fulfil them, I fear it will be long before men will begin the work of repentance, or engage in earnest in the practice of neglected duties.

Object. 5. In *Matth.* xxii. 11, 12. we read,—"When the king came in to see the guests, he saw there a man which had not on a wedding garment. And he said unto him, Friend, how camest thou in hither not having a wedding garment? and he was speechless."—Since he was blamed for coming in without a wedding garment, and had nothing to answer, it is argued that none have a warrant to come into the visible church without sanctifying grace.

I shall not avail myself of that common observation, that arguments founded on circumstances in parable are too precarious to be much depended on, since similitudes seldom hold in every circumstance: If we attend carefully to the parable itself, we shall find no foundation for this conclusion.

By the kingdom of heaven all agree that the church is to be understood; the supper signifies the privileges to which rightful and qualified members are admitted. The wedding garment is the qualification for these privileges. The man without it, is one who comes unqualified to partake of them, who when challenged for his presumption has nothing to answer, so is cast out.

But, is this feast on earth, or in heaven? Does it signify the privileges and enjoyments of the visible church here, or of the mystical church in the future state? The determination of this question must determine how the parable must be expounded.

Many understand the marriage feast of the blessedness of the heavenly state. The wedding garment must then mean the righteousness of the saints. The man without the wedding garment is one who, without this righteousness, comes to partake of the joys of heaven ; which is agreeable to what is elsewhere intimated, of some who at the day of judgment will come, and beg in vain to be admitted into heaven. The King's coming in to see the guests, is Christ's coming at the day of judgment. So Mr. Stoddard and Mr. Edwards both understand it. Then they who come to partake of the joys of heaven, without that holiness and righteousness without which no man shall see the Lord, will be reprimanded, silenced, and banished to outer darkness.

If this be the sense of the parable, it teaches us that the unsanctified shall not partake with true saints of the joys of heaven ; but it proves not that such cannot be rightful members of an instituted church, or lawfully come to special ordinances. When it was said to the man, How camest thou in hither without a wedding garment? the meaning cannot be, How camest thou into the instituted church, and to have external communion in ordinances without grace? He is not blamed for coming to ordinances without a warrant, but for coming to enjoy heavenly bliss without holiness. For, *First*. Many unconverted persons are rightfully members of the instituted church. They were born in it, and so brought in by God himself while graceless. These are not to be blamed for intruding into the house, if by the house we understand the visible church, however blameable they are for continuing graceless under the means they are favoured with.— *Secondly*. At the day of judgment there will be no visible instituted church, or outward ordinances for any to come to or be in. There will be no such house standing, no provision made therein for the entertainment of any. The coming of Christ will instantly dissolve all instituted churches, and abolish the outward ordinances. These tabernacles provided for our present accommodation will then be removed, with all their apparatus. It is not in the visible church that the heavenly feast is held, and into which the king comes at the day of judgment to see the guests, or where he sees the man without the wedding garment. That is impossible ; since the visible church will then be no more.—

Thirdly. The instituted church is the apartment into which men were invited and introduced by the servants to dress and prepare themselves for the heavenly feast, putting on the wedding garment of righteousness. It is by attending the ordinances given to the church that men are prepared for the blessedness of the heavenly state. Now though the unconverted are not prepared for heaven, this proves not that it is unwarrantable for such to use the means whereby they may become prepared, and attend the ordinances of the instituted church for that end. Some who are not inward saints, may yet be visible saints; and to such the ordinances are given.

But if we suppose the marriage feast to be held in the kingdom of heaven upon earth, that is in the instituted church, and to denote the outward ordinances and privileges there enjoyed, then the parable must be expounded conformably to this hypothesis: Thus—the Jews were first invited into the gospel church, but refused to come. Then the invitation was sent to the Gentiles, many of whom were gathered in. The wedding garment is the qualification for regular external communion, that is, visible saintship. The man without a wedding garment was a scandalous person, who contrary to the gospel rule had thrust himself in, though he was not a visible saint; so did not appear clothed in the livery of the king. The king coming in to see the guests signifies Christ visiting and inspecting his visible churches as their political head, which is done by the instrumentality of those who in his name are to maintain spiritual government in and over the house of God, and see that the ordinances of government and discipline are duly executed. Notice is taken of one who appears not in the garb of a credible profession, but had either cast it off, or at least was become scandalous, and so unfit for external communion. When called to an account he is convicted, and has nothing to answer. *Then the King said*, Christ by the gospel rule gave order (for Christ speaks in his visible church only by his written word)—He said *to his servants*, his ministers, to whom the keys of the kingdom of heaven are committed, who keep the doors of the house, and are authorized in his name to *bind* and *loose*: He said to them—*Bind him hand and foot*—lay him under censure—*take him away*—excommunicate him—*cast him into outer darkness.* Let him be as a heathen, as those who are in the darkness of infidelity, and subject to the spirit who rules in the children of darkness and disobedience. There shall be weeping and gnashing of teeth.*

If

---

* Mr. Henry has this note on the parable. " There is a binding in this world by the servants, the ministers, whose suspending of persons that walk disorderly

If the man without the wedding garment was ordered to be cast out of the visible church, as having no right to have external communion in ordinances, he was certainly a scandalous man, and excommunicated as such. For Christ gives no orders to his servants to cast any out of the visible church but those who are scandalous. But though scandalous persons ought not to come to church communion, this proves not that no unconverted persons may lawfully come. For some of these are visible saints, and not scandalous.

Object. 6. The covenant of grace is a covenant of salvation. How then can those who are not in a state of salvation be in the covenant, or have a right to any of its special privileges.

Answ. The covenant of grace contains a promise of salvation for true believers, who are interested therein in respect of its invisible administration. It has also grants of external privileges for visible saints, who are interested therein in respect of its external administration, as has been argued at large in discoursing on the covenant; and is, I think, generally acknowledged, tho' it seems to be forgotten by those who urge this objection. Now special ordinances being external covenant privileges, why may not visible saints have a right to use them, even supposing they are not saints in heart? And if a profession of faith morally sincere, constitutes a man a visible saint in the account of the church, and of his own conscience, this is the condition or qualification to which the gospel rule annexes a right to the ordinances in their outward administration.

Object. 7. Sacraments are seals of the covenant, not only for the confirmation of its truth, but also seals applied to the communicant as a party, appropriating the blessings of the covenant to him. How then can they rightfully belong to one who accepts not of the covenant, but rejects it?

Answer. It is true none have a right to the seals but they who are in the covenant. But visible saints are in the covenant, in its outward administration, though some are not in it so as to be entitled to its invisible saving blessings. Now the sacraments seal the covenant of grace, with all its privileges, promises and obligations to and upon those who are in covenant. But they seal according to the tenor of the covenant. Absolute promises and grants (including such as are become absolute by the fulfilment

---

disorderly to the scandal of religion is called binding them, Mat. xviii. 18. Bind them up from partaking of special ordinances, and the peculiar privileges of their church membership. Bind them over to the righteous judgment of God. Take him away. When the wickedness of hypocrites appears they are to be taken away from the communion of the faithful, to be cut off as withered branches." But I find no gospel rule interdicting the use of outward ordinances to visible saints because unconverted.

ment of their conditions) are absolutely sealed and confirmed to those to whom they belong. Thus the promises of pardon and salvation are absolutely sealed to believers. The grant or promise of external covenant privileges is sealed and appropriated absolutely to visible saints. Conditional promises are also sealed with a special application to those to whom the seal is applied; assuring them not absolutely that they shall receive the blessings promised, but that they in particular shall certainly receive them upon their complying with the condition. But the sacraments do not make conditional promises become absolute. Nor are they a seal or token given to the receiver, testifying that he has complied with the condition of all the promises, and so is absolutely entitled to them. In the administration of the sacrament we may conceive that Christ addresses every rightful communicant to this effect: "This covenant is sure and steadfast to you who are in and under it. It belongs to you; its bonds are on you. A compliance with its requirements is expected of you in particular. Whatever promises or grants you are entitled to, according to the tenor of the covenant, are sealed and confirmed absolutely to you. And all the conditional grants and promises are to you, and are your's upon your compliance with the conditions. As a solemn seal and token of this, take and eat this symbol, or memorial of my body broken for you, to purchase and seal this covenant—and drink ye all of this cup, as a pledge of the new covenant in my blood shed for you."

To apply the seal or token of the covenant to those who have no interest therein would indeed be like sealing a blank. But visible saints with their children are in the covenant, so far as to have a covenant right to the privileges pertaining to its external administration. And the sacraments are to them a seal of the covenant—*that* its duties are in a peculiar manner binding on them; *that* some at least of its grants belong to them absolutely; *that* its conditional offers are made especially to them, and shall be theirs, upon their acceptance of them, yea, if they do not positively reject them; and whether they comply or not with the conditions on which the saving grace of the covenant is proposed to their acceptance, yet the offer shall be continued to them so long as they continue visible saints; the privileges of the kingdom of God shall not be taken away, unless they put them away by a positive rejection: Finally, the indefinite promises of converting and sanctifying grace made absolutely to the visible church, are indefinitely sealed and confirmed to the members. And will any say that all this is a mere blank, a mere nothing?

The sacraments are not a seal to each communicant, that all the blessings of the covenant absolutely belong to him, whether he he accepts of them or not; or that *he has complied* with all the conditions, upon which all the blessings of the covenant are offered. They who so imagine deceive themselves. There are some covenant blessings to which many who are in the covenant, and even many true believers are not at present entitled, as not having yet performed the condition to which they are promised. Briefly then, the seals are a token to all those to whom they are rightfully applied: *That* the covenant is sure and steadfast, and its promises shall be fulfilled according to the true tenor of them: *That* as visible saints they have a covenant right to attend external ordinances, and enjoy the privileges of church members: *That* if they are, or shall become true believers, the spiritual blessings of the covenant are or shall be theirs: *That* if the sacraments or other ordinances are *worthily used*, they shall receive the spiritual benefit of them. But they are not applied as a seal or token from Christ to every *rightful* communicant, that he is a *worthy* communicant, or a true believer, or entitled absolutely to all covenant blessings. There is a difference between a *rightful* and a *worthy* attendance on ordinances. The Apostle disputes not the right of the Corinthians to come to the Lord's supper, though he blames them for coming unworthily.

Object. 8. The sacraments are also seals on the part of the receiver. As Christ in and by them gives an outward seal, or confirming token of the truth and stability of all the grants and promises of the covenant; so the communicant does on his part solemnly seal his acceptance of, and consent to the covenant. But this no unconverted person does in sincerity. And since it is unlawful for one falsely to profess, and then seal a consent to the covenant, the unconverted may not come to the sacraments.

Answer. It is granted, the sacrament may be considered as a seal on the part of the receiver; that is, a confirming token of profession. And as it is unlawful for any to profess in known hypocrisy, so it would be aggravated wickedness to seal such a profession at the Lord's supper. None may come to this ordinance, but those who may lawfully and warrantably exhibit such a profession as shall give them a right of admission. If no unconverted man can without lying make such a profession of religion as would entitle him to admission, it would be plainly unlawful for him to seal the same at the sacrament. But whoever professes in moral sincerity, does really assent and consent to the gospel, so far as he knows himself. He is not conscious of hypocrisy. He does not wilfully misrepresent his own sentiments. Now such a professor cannot be justly charged with lying; for a lie is a wilful misrepresentation.

I suppose

I suppose it will not be denied, that whoever finds not but that he does believe and consent to the gospel, may and ought thus to profess, though he may not be persuaded of his own godly sincerity, so does not and cannot profess or pretend that he is one of this character. I ask now, has such a professor a right of admission to the communion of the church?

If he ought to be admitted upon such a profession, then he has a warrant to seal this his profession at the Lord's supper: For all who have a warrant to profess that which gives a right of admission, have a right to come and seal the same.

But if such a professor is not to be admitted unless he withal declare absolutely, that he is a sincere christian, if this be the profession which gives a right of admission, and is to be sealed with the sacrament, no one can lawfully thus profess, if he has the least doubt of his own sincerity. For we may not absolutely assert any thing for truth, of which we have any doubt.

Object. 9. What has been offered in answer to this objection, may also serve to obviate the objection from the nature and significancy of sacramental actions: That in receiving the sacrament the communicant makes a solemn profession of faith, love, gratitude and cordial subjection to Christ, which no unsanctified man can truly make. The sacrament may indeed be termed, as was said, a seal, or ratifying token of our christian profession. But the sacramental actions are not so to be interpreted as to signify or imply any thing more than is contained in that profession to which they are annexed; especially, as I find no such interpretation given in the scriptures. Now the profession, upon which the primitive christians came and were received into the church, was not a profession of assurance, or confidence in their own godliness, but of faith in Christ as the Saviour and Lord, the sincerity of which was afterwards to be proved and manifested by its fruits. And though in receiving the sacramental elements we do profess to receive Christ, and hope for salvation only through him, and according to the tenor of the new covenant, and that without known reserve or hypocrisy; yet care should be taken that this be not so understood as, if *a profession of knowing our own hearts*, or having a persuasion that we are saints in heart, was meant to be wrapped up, and implied in this our profession: For this would lay a block in the way, and a snare on the conscience of the weak and doubting; who must either neglect the duty and privilege which belongs to them as visible saints, or presume on making a profession, the truth of which they doubt.

It is also still to be remembered, that the question is not, *whether an unsanctified man ever does, while such come to, and attend gospel ordinances worthily,* so as to have a *covenant right* to the spiritual

ritual benefit of them. We grant, that no such person is in a present capacity to eat and drink in the manner he ought, at the Lord's table, or to attend any other of the instituted means of religion. Yet this proves not but that a visible saint, though unconverted, may as lawfully use the special ordinances granted by Christ to the visible church, when he can do it without known hypocrisy, as attend any ordinances, or do any other action which he has an acknowledged right to do. Nor does any thing appear to bar his right of acting in one case, more than the other. At the same time it is certain that none are allowed to profane any divine ordinance, by using it in an unworthy manner. It should therefore be the serious concern of every one to attend every ordinance, and do every thing with the spirit, the principles and aims of a sincere christian.

Object. 10. Those have no fitness in themselves to come to the privileges of the church, who, if they were known, would not be fit to be admitted by others. But unsanctified men, if they were known to be such, would be unfit to be admitted, and so have no right to come.

I answer. What gives any one a right, and in that respect a fitness to be admitted to church privileges is credible evidence of grace. Now they who are known to be unsanctified want evidence of grace: For it is impossible that one who exhibits credible evidence of grace should be known to be graceless, unless by supernatural revelation. But it is not the want of grace, but the want of credible evidence of grace which renders one unfit for admission. So whoever knows himself to be unsanctified, wants those evidences of sanctification which would give him a right or warrant, and in that respect a fitness, to come for the privileges of the church; since it is impossible for one who finds credible evidence of sanctification in himself, or who is morally sincere in professing christianity, to know, except by supernatural revelation, that he is graceless. But it is not the want of grace, but the want of this evidence of grace, which renders him unfit, as wanting a right or warrant to come. For though credible evidences of grace do not make it certain that a man is a true saint, yet they make it certain that he has a right of admission, and a warrant to come for church privileges, as we have before argued at large, and is acknowledged by those who have most objected to the right of unsanctified men to the sacraments. Thus Mr. Baxter, who opposed Mr. Blake, yet says expressly, " He who can say I am not certain that I truly repent, but as far as I know my heart I do, is not to be hindered from the sacrament by that uncertainty." And Mr. Edwards, who opposed Mr. Stoddard's principle, says, " The best judgment we can form after all proper endeavours to know the truth, *muſt* govern and determine us," plainly acknowledging that it is our right and duty to conduct ourſelves according to it. Dr. Mather too, while diſputing againſt Mr. Stoddard, ſays, " If after ſerious ſelf-examination, a man cannot but hope he is a godly man, he *may* come, though he hath not aſſurance ;" that is, he *may* come *lawfully*, or has a right or warrant to come. And all our divines and caſuiſts ſeem to be of the ſame judgment; tho' many ſeem not to have conſidered that this is in effect an acknowledgment of the right of ſome unſanctified men to come to the ſacrament: For I think none will ſay, that all who ſee reaſon to hope that they are converted are ſincere chriſtians.

Object. 11. If graceleſs perſons who are morally ſincere may come to communion, the greateſt part of communicants are like to be not only graceleſs, but void of moral ſincerity. For moral ſincerity, without grace, commonly ſoon vaniſhes; and yet theſe if not ſcandalous, muſt continue in the church even without moral ſincerity.

I anſwer. Moral ſincerity in profeſſing chriſtianity is a credible evidence of ſanctification. Credible evidence gives a right of admiſſion and acceſs. Whenever this evidence fails, the right annexed to it becomes void. If any one is viſibly unfit for communion, according to the rule of the goſpel, he is to be debarred. If any one finds himſelf unfit, the rule forbids his coming. If he will come notwithſtanding, it is no fault in the rule, but the fault is wholly in thoſe who tranſgreſs it. If neither the church nor the profeſſor find any unfitneſs, he ought not to be debarred, or refrain from coming. The goſpel rule was never deſigned or calculated to keep thoſe out of the church who *appear not* to be unfit for communion, be their inward ſtate what it may.

I would humbly wiſh thoſe who thus object to conſider calmly what rule they would have for chriſtians to try themſelves by, in order to determine whether they may come to ordinances. Would they have none come but ſuch as have certain evidence of ſanctification? No. Would they have thoſe come who find credible evidence, or reaſons to hope they are ſincere? This is the rule we contend for? Will they ſay that moral ſincerity in the profeſſion of chriſtianity is not a credible evidence of ſanctifying grace? I conceive that it is as good evidence as can ordinarily be exhibited in any profeſſion, as has been argued. Would they have a rule which, if duly obſerved, the *greater part* of church members ſhould be true ſaints? Who can ſay but that the greater part of thoſe who profeſs chriſtianity unconſcious of hypocriſy are ſuch? But if the door of the viſible church is not ſo narrow but that ſome unconverted may go in, who can ſay whether the greater part of thoſe who enter are of this character? What terms of
communion

communion, which any unsanctified man can come up to, will certainly secure a greater number of true saints in any church? However, if any unsanctified persons can come into the church according to the rule of the gospel, they have in the sight of God a right to come. If the rule allows none to come but true saints, what right have we to tell any whose saintship is doubtful, that they *may* and *must* come?

Object. 12. I shall mention but one objection more. Christians are directed to examine themselves in coming to the table of the Lord, whether they are the subjects of sanctifying grace. We must then conclude that the Apostle would not have them come, unless they find themselves true saints.

I shall not repeat what others have said to obviate this objection. Admitting the sense here given, that christians should, when coming to the Lord's supper, examine the state and frame of their souls, whether they have the faith, and repentance, the graces and virtues of true christians in habit and exercise, it makes no difficulty. We constantly suppose that christians not only ought to exercise the graces of the christian temper when they come, and that they cannot otherwise attend worthily upon ordinances, so as to have a covenant right to the spiritual benefit of them, but that they ought to have credible evidence in their own consciences that they believe in Christ, repent of sin, and resolve without delay to live in obedience to the commandments of God. And that those who have not reason to hope they are sincere ought not to reproach that holy ordinance, in which they are to seal a professed consent to the covenant. And that a serious examination of themselves is a fit mean of their judging their spiritual state, and discerning the reasons of hope that are in them, and the right they have to the privileges of christian communion. And if upon examining ourselves we find such evidences of christian piety, as I suppose every one who can profess christianity in moral sincerity may and must be conscious of, we may conclude that we have *certainly* a right and warrant to come to the Lord's supper, whatever doubts may still remain respecting our state. For it is not the certainty of inward sanctification, but the reality of hopeful and credible evidence thereof in our own conscience, that is the foundation of our right and warrant.

Other objections might have been mentioned, but these which have been noticed seem to be some of the most considerable. I have also in this discourse often had my eye upon objections and difficulties, endeavouring to obviate them without calling them up to view.

SECTION

SECTION III.

Reconciling Remarks.

UPON the whole view of the case before us, I humbly conceive that the difference of opinion between Christians, who have appeared with so much zeal on different sides of the question, not without some hard thoughts of each other, has not really been so wide, and by no means of so much importance as has often been thought.

All acknowledge that certain evidences of sanctification are not necessary to give one a right to church privileges; and that credible grounds of hope are a rational and sufficient warrant for a professor to come, and the church to receive him. That none are to be admitted but those for whom the church ought to have charity. None may come but those who can without known hypocrisy profess a serious and hearty assent and consent to the gospel. All the difference with respect to the *rule of admission* I think is this— The one says none are to be admitted but *such as are judged* to be true saints, making *the judgment of the church* the foundation or condition of the proponant's right to admission. The other maintains, that those are to be admitted who give credible evidence that they are true saints in a judgment of charity. So with respect to the *rule of conscience,* determining a right of access. The one says that none may come but such as *judge* themselves to be saints in heart, at least that this is most probable. The other thinks that however men may suspect, and even have a prevailing fear that their hearts are not right; yet if they find this evidence of sincerity, that their hearts condemn them not of hypocrisy, their warrant is good whether *the credit they give,* or the *confidence they have* in the reasons of their hope be more or less.

Now, while I cannot but hold with the latter, and think the other opinion pressed with difficulties which I know not how to remove, *viewing the matter in theory or speculation,* yet considered in reference to practice, the difference seems not to be of so great importance. Upon the former principle christians will indeed often be obliged to act with uncomfortable doubt and uncertainty whether they have a lawful right to do, what yet they may not and dare not neglect, so cannot act with the safety, freedom, and security of a sure and clear conscience; and so are in danger of sinning even in doing their duty, because they cannot do it in faith, that is, with a clear satisfaction and persuasion of conscience that it is their duty and right. But if they do not feel the jar of contradiction

tradiction when they are told that they may and must often act without a certain right to act; that they may be satisfied they must to come to ordinances, before they are satisfied of their duty and right to come to them, though this seems not the right way of removing doubts, yet it is hoped that christians will not be kept back from their duty by their scruples.

Indeed I cannot but think the greater part at least of those who hold that none have a right to the sacraments but true saints, differ little in sentiment from their brethren, who think that visible saints have a right to them. For they who connect this *right* with inward sanctification, yet constantly suppose it is the evidence of this alone which gives one *a warrant* to come, and the church *a right* to receive him. So that the right which grace is supposed to give seems to be a kind of dormant potential quality, of which no use can be made, till it be credibly manifested. This supposed right in the sight of God is not of itself any *warrant*, or sufficient *reason* for coming into church communion. And many who greatly doubt whether they are the subjects of sanctifying grace, may yet be bound in conscience to come, as being fully persuaded upon good grounds that it is most reasonable for them to do so. Such evidence of grace as leaves it uncertain whether a man is a true saint, and which it is therefore supposeable, may be found in some who are not saints in heart, may it seems, by the acknowledgment of our brethren, give him *a certain warrant to come* and the church to receive him, in which I see not but that they agree with us. So that this *right in the sight of God*, which they would connect with the truth of grace, seems to be only a speculative notion of no use. *It is a right without a warrant.* A notion calculated not at all to keep unqualified persons out of the church, but only to breed perplexing scruples in the consciences of many who yet it is acknowledged ought not to be kept back. It lays many professors under a sad necessity either of absenting from the communion of saints, when they have confessedly more reason to come, and are bound in conscience and duty to do so, or else to come with a doubting conscience. And which part of the alternative soever they take, they are under a necessity of wounding their conscience; from which they cannot escape, till they are fully persuaded in their own mind that they may lawfully do what is to be done. If those who find reason to hope they are sincere may and ought to come to the sacraments, let us not lay snares for their consciences, by saying it is doubtful whether or no they may and ought to come; since their right depends on something of doubtful reality. If we have any rights in the sight of God which is inevident to us, we may rely on his faithfulness that he will not fail of fulfilling his gracious promise. But to make our right and warrant to use ordinances depend on this, will leave us no rule we can act by.

Though christians are often in doubt as to their spiritual state, yet if they duly attend to their rule, the path of duty is plainly described. They need not stay till they are satisfied of their own godly sincerity, before they can know that it is their duty and right to walk in the commandments and ordinances of the Lord. While the conscience is doubtful, we cannot act with safety, or with a good conscience. But as soon as we are satisfied what is most reasonable for us to do, the doubt is then resolved, the conscience is sure, our right and duty is plain. And we shall shew ourselves unskilful guides, if we infuse doubts and scruples, by telling men, that though it is plainly most reasonable, and they may and must do so, or so, yet it is uncertain whether it is lawful for them to do it. This inconvenience and inconsistency we can avoid, while we maintain that it is the evidence, and not the reality of grace which gives a lawful right to gospel ordinances. Nor need any christian, however doubtful of his spiritual state, have his conscience insnared with doubts whether he has a right to do that which must and ought to be done by him. But if we hold that none but true saints have a right or warrant to come to ordinances, I see not how we can consistently extricate doubting christians from the perplexity, jeopardy, and necessity of sinning in which they must find themselves entangled since they can neither act nor forbear without presumption.

But when I consider the rules and counsels given for the direction and relief of christians under these doubts, and that all agree in encouraging and urging an attendance on the ordinances upon all who can sincerely consent to the covenant, so far as they know themselves, I am much confirmed in my persuasion, that sober and moderate men on each side of the question differ very little from each other in their true aim, however they may not be alike clear and consistent in their theories, or exact in their expressions.

Perhaps there may be some difference of opinion upon this question, Whether any besides true saints have *a title by covenant grant* to the ordinances of the gospel? It seems to be agreed, that some whose character as true saints is uncertain, may have sufficient reason, and therefore a warrant to come to them, as has been observed. But it may still be thought by some that true saints only have *a passive right*, or *covenant title* to them.

As to the inward virtue and sanctifying efficacy of ordinances, all will agree that none have a *covenant title* to this, but those who worthily attend upon them. But that the ordinances in the outward

ward administration are granted *by the covenant* to the *visible church*, is a doctrine commonly and expresly taught in the reformed churches, and I find not that it has been expresly denied by any. Thus, in the Westminster confession of faith, " Unto this visible church (consisting of those that profess the true religion, together with their children) Christ hath given the ministry oracles and ordinances of God." And our divines, Cotton, Hooker, Shepard, express themselves very fully to the same purpose, alledging the words of the Apostle in proof, asserting that the oracles of God were committed to the Jews as *a covenant privilege*: Yea, what principle is more generally taught' and professed by Pædobaptists, than that the children of regular church members are in the covenant, and have a right or title by covenant to special privileges? But if any suppose that the ordinances are *granted by covenant only to true saints*, and that they only have properly a *covenant title* to them; yet while it is granted that some whose title is uncertain may be bound in reason and conscience, and so have *a warrant to come* to them, a difference of opinion in such a speculative nicety may be indulged, without hard thoughts of each other.

CHAP. VII.

Of a RIGHT *to a* BLESSING *with* ORDINANCES.

SECTION I.

THERE remains yet another case or question relative to a right to church privileges, which was proposed to be considered; and that is, who have a covenant right to the spiritual benefit and sanctifying virtue of the ordinances, in and by their attending to the outward administration of them? But there seems to be little difficulty or difference of judgment on this point.

There are some who have an acknowledged right of admission and access to ordinances, who may yet use them in such a manner as to have no covenant right, or reasonable ground to expect the acceptance or blessing of Christ therein. They may so abuse and profane

fane gofpel inftitutions as to expofe themfelves to the judgments of God. This feems to have been the cafe of fome in the Corinthian church, whofe intemperance, uncharitablenefs, and diforderly behaviour, at the table of the Lord, the Apoftle reproves. He does not blame them for coming without a right, but for coming and behaving in an improper manner. This cafe then fhould not be confounded with either of the foregoing, but is to be confidered by itfelf, and determined by rules and maxims fuited to it. We cannot argue that becaufe a man ought not to come unworthily, therefore he may not come, or be admitted; or on the other hand, that every one has a prefent or immediate right to the privileges of chriftian communion, provided he will ufe them in a right manner. For then neither the church, nor the perfon coming to communion, could know beforehand whether he had a right to the ordinances, fince his right would depend upon a future unknown contingency.

To the queftion then, who have a right to the fanctifying virtue of ordinances, and the bleffing of Chrift from them, I would fay in brief, that the fpiritual efficacy of ordinances is by the covenant annexed to *a right and worthy ufe of them*. I fhall not here enquire what is implied in a worthy attendance, which has been often and well difcourfed of by practical writers; but would obferve in general, *that* unfanctified men always fail in the manner of their attendance, fo as that they have no covenant title to the faving benefit of them: *That* this may alfo fometimes be the cafe of true chriftians: And *that* the beft have always reafon to be humbled for their imperfections, and the unfuitable manner in which they perform holy duties; but yet all who are able to ufe gofpel ordinances, with a meafure of godly fincerity, fhall receive a bleffing therein, and be gracioufly accepted.

It is the bleffing of Chrift, and the working of the holy Spirit, which gives gofpel ordinances their virtue, efficacy and quickening energy. This bleffing pertains to the inward, invifible adminiftration of the covenant, which is wholly and immediately in the hands of Chrift. And none are entitled to it but thofe who are inwardly fanctified; and even thefe have not a covenant right thereto, any further than they are enabled rightly and worthily to ufe the ordinances, which requires actual fupplies of grace in time of need. And though this needed affiftance is promifed in general to all true faints, yet there is much of fovereignty exercifed in the adminiftration of it. Some receive it in much larger meafures than others; and the fame perfons find the fpirit helping their infirmities more fenfibly, and in a greater degree at fome times than at others—of which we can often give no other account than this, that God worketh in us to will and to do according

cording to his good pleasure. But Christ has not so restrained himself, but that he often adds a blessing to his ordinances, making them savingly profitable to those who have not come to them, and attended to the administration of them in the manner they ought. Though ordinances do not confer grace *ex opere operato*, yet those who *rightfully* attend upon them, may hope for a blessing by means of them, notwithstanding such actual unfitness as bars them not from lawful access; and though the manner of their attendance may be such that they are not entitled by promise to a blessing: For Christ often dispenses unpromised, as well as promised blessings by means of his ordinances, which should encourage those who lawfully may, to come to them, however unfit they may seem to attend upon them in a due and worthy manner.

SECTION II.

Of the Sin and Danger of attending Unworthily.

IT may be asked whether the sin and danger of coming to and attending holy ordinances unworthily, be not greater than that of refraining from them; and consequently, whether they who have not reason to think it at least most probable that they shall attend upon them worthily, ought not rather to be kept back through fear of aggravating their guilt and misery, than to come upon the presumption, that through sovereign unpromised grace they may receive a blessing.

I answer. The greater sin and danger in cases of this kind depends on circumstances which may be infinitely various; so that it may not be possible to lay down general rules for determining that sins of one kind are greater than sins of another, which will hold without exception. Nor is this a matter of much practical importance to us, since we are not allowed to chuse any sin however small, to avoid the danger of any sin however great. We may not neglect any duty for fear we should perform it unworthily, and thereby incur greater guilt; but should set about the practice of it, and endeavour to do it in a right manner. Nor may we be negligent of the manner in which we perform religious duties, or allow ourselves in an unworthy manner of attending to them, as thinking that this is a less sin than it would be to neglect duties altogether; but resolve and strive by divine grace to avoid the sin and danger on either hand. We may not neglect the means of religion for fear of using them unworthily, and that then they will not be blessed to us, but will operate to our hurt.

hurt. Nor should we think that a bare outward attendance will give us reason to expect a blessing, if we indulge hypocrisy, and aim not to approve ourselves to God.

The ordinances cannot be worthily and rightly attended without the exercise of grace. And it should be the desire, aim, and hope of all when coming to them, to use the means of grace in godly sincerity, that so they may receive a blessing. Their encouragement to come should not be an imagination that any can rightly and acceptably attend upon them, or have a covenant right to the spiritual benefit of them without true faith, and the graces of sanctification; but a hope, that through the grace of Christ they shall be enabled to act with the spirit, the principles, the aims, and sincerity of true christians, and by waiting on God renew their strength. But it is not necessary that we be satisfied beforehand, that we shall attend ordinances in a worthy and acceptable manner, and receive the spiritual blessing thereto annexed, in order to our having a clear warrant, and sufficient encouragement to come to them. Many true saints are not satisfied of their own sincerity: And they who have clear and good evidence know not what frames they may be in, when they address themselves to the performance of religious duties; and whether they shall be blessed and accepted therein. We are not of ourselves sufficient to think or do any thing worthily as of ourselves, but all our sufficiency is of God. And will any say that they can advance any claims upon him to furnish them with future supplies of actual grace, which shall effectually secure them from the power of temptation, and indwelling corruption, and keep their graces so in exercise as that they shall rightly and worthily perform the duties before them. We know that we shall fail in all the duties of religion we engage in; and we know not how far God may leave us to miscarry therein: Yet this is no reason why we should neglect duties; which would be running ourselves immediately into sin, to secure ourselves from the danger or possibility of perhaps a less sin.

So if a man finds reason to fear that he is not a saint in heart, and if this is really the case, this is no reason why he should neglect any duties and means of religion enjoined upon, or appointed for him, lest he should by an undue manner of attendance, enhance his sin and misery. For it is not certain, whatever his present state may be, but that he may perform the duty in sincerity. He may in the very act come under the sanctifying influence of divine grace; yea, there is more reason to hope for this, while he is seriously waiting upon God in those ordinances by which he is wont to draw and turn the hearts of men to himself, and make them his willing people in the day of his power.

If he sets himself to perform the duties, and attend ordinances of religion enjoined upon him, there is a possibility, yea reason to hope, that however unfit and uncapable he may seem at present to do any thing in a holy and acceptable manner, God may visit his soul with the needed influence of his grace, and so supply whatever was wanting to render his doings acceptable. But a sinful omission and neglect of duty cannot be sanctified. So that, as was said before, to neglect duty for fear of doing it unworthily would be to chuse a certain and perhaps greater evil, rather an uncertain possibility and danger of that which, if it should happen, may not be so bad.

If we desire and endeavour to do what we are commanded, and have a right to do as visible saints, that is, attend gospel ordinances, and can do it without known hypocrisy, what reason have we to conclude that we are not sincere? And admitting that we are not, what reason have we to conclude that God may not make us sincere while attending the common means of grace, rather than in neglecting them? And at any rate, what reason have we to think that it is more sinful and dangerous to attend gospel ordinances, which we are bound and have a lawful right to do, though we should fail in the manner of our attendance, than it would be to neglect them, for fear that we should fail in the manner, and not use them worthily? Is it the safest and most hopeful way to avoid enhancing our guilt, and obtain the blessings of divine grace, for men to act contrary to the dictates of their own reason and conscience, and withdraw themselves from the means by which God ordinarily conveys the blessings of his grace?

It will be very generally allowed, that those who are favoured with gospel ordinances, which are common instituted means of conversion to sinners, as well as of edifying saints, may and ought to come to them, whether they are converted or unconverted; and that the blessing of Christ may be hoped for to accompany the dispensation of the word, and prayer for saving good to such as may not attend on these ordinances in a holy manner. They who would restrain a right to sacraments only to true saints, have yet strongly and constantly maintained that it is lawful, and the duty of the unconverted to attend the means of conversion.*

But

---

* " Socrates might pray to God, and he attended his duty when he did so, although he knew not the revelation which God had made of himself in his word. Seneca, though he did not embrace the gospel, which at that day was preached in the world, yet he might pray to that supreme Being, whom he acknowledged. And if his brother Galio at Corinth, when Paul

But it has been thought that the sin and danger of coming to the Lord's supper unworthily, as the unconverted do, if they come at all, is much greater than that of coming while unconverted to other ordinances, which are the instituted means of conversion: That it is absolutely unlawful to come at all, unless they eat and drink worthily: That this not being a converting ordinance, nor designed for the use of any unconverted, there is no reason to hope such will receive any spiritual benefit from it; but we have reason to expect that they will eat and drink judgment to themselves. Since then no good is to be hoped for, and great evil and danger to be expected from an unconverted man's using this ordinance, there is need of peculiar caution; and it must be desperate rashness and presumption for any to venture, unless they are well satisfied that they are true saints, and shall approach and partake worthily at the table of the Lord.

It is to be observed, that this objection supposes or admits all that has hitherto been argued and pleaded for, viz. that the unconverted may be regular church members, visible saints have a right of admission, be bound in conscience and reason to come, that they may have a right to ordinances by a covenant grant, &c. These things having been before discussed, are now taken for granted; and the question before us comes to this, whether, if

all

Paul preached there, had prayed to this supreme Being to guide him into the truth, that he might know whether the doctrine Paul preached was true, he therein would have acted very becoming a reasonable creature, and any one would have acted unreasonably in forbidding him. But yet surely neither of these men was qualified for the christian sacraments. So that it is apparent there is and ought to be a distinction made between duties of worship, with respect to qualifications for them. Any natural man may as well express his desires to God, as hear when God declares his will to him. 'Tis true when an unconverted man prays, the manner of his doing it is sinful."

Edwards' Humble Enquiry, p. 114, 115.

" They who have no interest in the covenant of grace, and are in no respect God's covenant people, may lawfully hear the word and pray."

Idem. Answer to Williams, p. 107.

" If a man at his own cost sets up a school in order to teach ignorant children to read, and accordingly ignorant children should go thither in order to learn to read, would he come into the school and say in anger to an ignorant child that he found there, How camest thou in hither before thou hadst learnt to read? Did the Apostle Paul ever rebuke the Heathen, who came to hear him preach the gospel, saying, How came you hither to hear me preach, not having grace? This would have been unreasonable; because preaching is an ordinance appointed to that end that men might obtain grace. Can we suppose that Christ will say to men in indignation at the day of judgment, How came you to presume to use the means I appointed for your conversion before you were converted?"

Idem. Answer to Williams, p. 133.

all that has hitherto been argued for be admitted, yet the great sin, guilt, and danger which an unconverted person incurs by coming unworthily to the Lord's supper, when it is considered that no benefit can be reasonably hoped for by such a one which might compensate and counterbalance this hazzard; whether this would not make it unwarrantable rashness for such as are not well persuaded of their own sincerity to come to this ordinance?

To the several particulars here alledged I would reply: *In the first place*, it is granted *that* the unconverted cannot, while such, come to and partake of the Lord's supper *in a holy manner*, and that, in this sense, such come unworthily, and have no covenant right to a blessing; *that* the sinful manner of their approach renders them obnoxious, as all sin does, to God's displeasure. But this proves not that it is more unlawful for them to come to the Lord's table, than to hear or read the word, to pray, to eat their own bread, or voluntarily forbear to do any of these things. And yet it is acknowledged *that* sinners may pray, and attend the means of instruction and conversion; and that herein they "attend to their duty, and act very becoming a reasonable creature." *That* they are not to be blamed or charged with presumption for "using the means of conversion before they are converted; tho' they do none of these things in a holy manner, but do every thing unworthily in this sense: So that the reason seems to be at least as strong against neglecting ordinances unworthily, as coming to them unworthily: It is of no more weight on one side than on the other, and therefore proves nothing.

Secondly. The fault which the Apostle reproves in the Corinthians, and terms eating and drinking unworthily, appears not to have been coming to the ordinance while unconverted. But it was their disorderly carriage at the Lord's table, which seems to have been very gross and scandalous, and such as few serious and conscientious professors, after having had the advantage of being duly instructed in the nature and design of the ordinance, would be likely to fall into. And yet the Apostle does not suggest to them that he judged them to be unconverted. Nor need we judge thus of them, though probably some of them might not be sincere. We have reason, however, to think that many who are not saints in heart, are not guilty of the disorderly behaviour at the Lord's table, here reproved as unworthy eating and drinking, not discerning the Lord's body. That is, as expositors generally understand the words, not distinguishing from a common meal this religious feast commemorative of, and representing the Lord's body. And though the unconverted are unworthy communicants, in the sense lately mentioned, yet if they attend the ordinance in a serious and religious remembrance of Christ, thus making difference between it and their common food, they seem not to be chargeable with the sin of eating and drinking unworthily in the sense more directly intended by the Apostle in this place. But,

Thirdly. Whether the sin of coming to the Lord's supper unworthily be greater and more dangerous, than to pray, or hear, or read the word unworthily cannot, I conceive, be determined in general without taking into consideration the circumstances by which the one or the other may be aggravated, or alleviated. Some may profane divine ordinances in such a manner by an unworthy attendance on them, that it would have been a less sin, if they had not come to them. In others, a neglect of them may be more sinful and dangerous than an undue manner of attendance. The views, tempers, and manner with which some pray, or hear the word, may be more displeasing to God, and dangerous to their own souls, than the views, aims, and manner of some when they come unworthily to the Lord's table. We cannot conclude, if a man has partaken unworthily, that his sin would have been less if he had withdrawn. Perhaps turning his back upon the ordinance, which it was his right and duty to attend, might have been a yet greater sin. Though the Apostle blames the Corinthians for eating and drinking unworthily, yet he does not say it would have been less sinful, if they had neglected to come to the ordinance.

Fourthly. Suppose it be a greater and more dangerous sin to partake unworthily at the Lord's supper, than not to come to it, this is no sufficient reason for any one to absent himself, if it be his right and duty to come. It ought indeed to make him solicitous to come in a right manner, to labour to be actually prepared, to keep his heart with all diligence, looking earnestly to God for the aids of his grace, that his spirit may help his infirmity, and carry him through the solemn duty before him, and keep him from profaning the holy ordinance, and so bringing guilt and danger upon himself. But for any one to decline doing his duty, and using his privilege, thinking that this would be less sinful and dangerous than it would be to fail in the manner of attending to it, would be, as was said, to do what is in itself sinful, in order to prevent a future sin, which we fear will be more dangerous; which is what no one is allowed to do. Be the danger ever so great in our apprehension, we may not think to avoid it by doing any thing which is forbidden, or declining to do any thing which is enjoined upon us. We may not chuse a present sin, to preclude a future danger. And since it is certainly sinful for regular church members allowedly to neglect coming to the Lord's fupper, they may not do fo whatever their inward ftate may be. This rule, I conceive, will ftand upon firm grounds, though it were fupppofed that there were no reafon to hope that attending to the Lord's fupper would be of any fpiritual benefit to an unconverted church member, but would rather increafe his guilt and danger. We may not do evil to prevent evil.

SECTION III.

Whether the Lord's Supper be a Converting Ordinance.

AS the fuppofition, that there is no reafon to hope that the Lord's fupper will be of any fpiritual benefit to an unconverted communicant is grounded upon this principle, that this ordinance is not an inftituted means of converfion; it may not be amifs to examine this point a little further. For though we may fee that it is not of much practical importance, yet as it has been a fubject of debate among chriftians, I fhall take liberty, before I withdraw my hand from the table, to fhew my opinion.

It is not denied but that receiving the Lord's fupper may be the occafion of their converfion who have unwarrantably come and partaken of it. God fometimes makes the wickednefs of men, the occafion of good to them. But none will fay that the Lord's fupper is properly an inftituted mean of fpiritual good to thofe who are not allowed to come to it. It is not pretended by any, that this is a converting ordinance to any while out of the vifible church. None may lawfully partake but rightful church members. Now that fome rightful members may be unconverted, and being in and under the covenant as externally adminiftered, may have a covenant right to the outward ordinances, and be bound in duty, and have a good warrant to come to the Lord's fupper, having been before argued at large, is here fuppofed: and the queftion is, whether the Lord's fupper be an inftituted means of converfion to fuch rightful communicants as are unconverted?

According to this way of ftating the queftion, it appears that all arguments for the negative from the unlawfulnefs of an unfanctified man's coming to the facraments are precluded, as having been already confidered and anfwered. All agree that the Lord's fupper is not a converting ordinance to thofe who have no right and warrant to come to it. So that the point of enquiry is, whether, if we admit the right and duty of fome unfanctified men to come to the facrament, we have reafon to think it may be an inftituted mean of their converfion? Now,

Now, I must confess that I am not able to prove from the scriptures that the Lord's supper is a converting ordinance to the unconverted. I find not that this is asserted in the New Testament; or that it can be certainly inferred from any of the doctrines or facts there recorded. Neither do I find that the contrary is proveable by scripture: So that we seem not to have sufficient evidence certainly to determine the problem one way or the other. And what some have argued from experience, and from instances of persons who have been first savingly converted by means of their partaking of this ordinance seems not very conclusive. For I think the truth of the fact can scarce be made certain. And admitting the fact, that some may have been converted while attending on this ordinance, this will scarce make it certain, that their receiving the sacrament was the means of this happy change. For we cannot conclude that all the concomitant circumstances or occasions of any event have any proper efficiency as causes or means of producing it.

But on the other hand there are several considerations, which if they do not amount to a certain proof, yet seem to make it very credible, that the Lord's supper may be a converting ordinance to such regular and rightful communicants as are unconverted. For as such communicants need converting grace, I see not why we may not conceive that this ordinance may be designed to be a means of spiritual good to them as well as others. It seems rational to think that all gospel ordinances are instituted means of good to all characters of men who are proper and rightful subjects of them, and who need and are capable of receiving spiritual benefit from them. And if we consider this ordinance in its own nature, I see not but that it may be well adapted to subserve the first conversion of sinners, and promote penetential sorrow for sin in them, and cause them to mourn for it, while looking on him whom they have pierced, and by faith behold the Lamb of God, who taketh away the sin of the world, and who is evidently set forth as crucified before them. Why does it not appear to be as well fitted to be a means of their conversion, as other institutions which are acknowledged to be converting ordinances? Besides, I think none will doubt but that the Lord's supper may be, and often is a converting ordinance to declining saints; the mean of healing their backslidings, of reviving and advancing the work of repentance and conversion in them. Conversion is a gradual work. It is going on, and renewed day by day; though it is in an instant that we begin to be sincere. And it is allowed that the after exercises of repentance and turning to God are of the same kind for substance in christians with what they experience at their first conversion.

conversion. Now if the Lord's supper be a fit means of effecting and promoting the work of conversion in saints, why may it not be a fit means of effecting a work of the same kind in the unconverted? Or can any good reason be given, why these should be thought less capable or fit to be led to repentance by this than by other means?

Upon the whole, though I pretend not positively to determine any thing without more clear scriptural evidence, yet I see not but that the Lord's supper may be, by the blessing of God, the means of conversion to such rightful communicants as need converting grace: And that we may hope they will receive spirtual benefit from it. And however, that there appears no harm or danger in this opinion.

SECTION IV.

Objections Considered.

BUT it is objected, If the Lord's supper be a converting ordinance, what good reason can be given why none should come or be admitted to it, but such as there is reason to think are converted already? If a hospital were provided and furnished for nourishing the healthy, and healing the sick, would it not be unaccountable and unreasonable, if the officers were ordered not to admit any but such as they had reason to think were well?

Answer. If there be any weight in this objection it will prove that no ordinances are appointed as means of conversion to visible saints, and members of instituted churches; since none are to be admitted, or to come into church communion, but such as the church has reason to have charity for. And is it then thought absurd and unreasonable, that means of conversion should be provided and designed for the benefit of those, of whom there is reason to hope that they are converted? Will any say that no means of conversion are provided or instituted for church members, or that they have less reason than others to hope to be benefited by them? This would be a new doctrine indeed, never before heard in the church, which has always believed and taught that all gospel ordinances are granted by covenant to the visible church: "That church members enjoy many privileges which others enjoy not, and if not regenerated, are in a more likely way to obtain regenerating grace, and all the spiritual blessings both of the covenant and seal." [Cambridge platform, Chap. 12.]

Mr.

Mr. Shepard spoke the sense of the New-England churches in the following memorable words : " Others hear the word, but those in outward covenant enjoy it by covenant and promise : And hence these in the first place and principally are sought after by these means. And therefore Christ forbids his disciples at first to go preach in the way of the Gentiles, (persons out of covenant) but to the lost sheep of the house of Israel. And though he bids his disciples go preach to all nations, yet it is said, Acts iii. 26, " Unto you *first* hath he sent Christ, because you are the children of the promise and covenant. Repent therefore and be converted. Do not resist or refuse Christ : For he [God] hath first sent Christ to you, to bless you, and turn you from your iniquities. And hence it is that though the word may come to heathens, as well as church members, yet it comes not to them by way of covenant, as it doth to church members ; nor have they any promise of mercy aforehand, as church members have ; nor is it chiefly belonging to such, but unto the children of the covenant.*" And not only are gospel ordinances in a peculiar manner the privileges of visible churches and saints, as well converting ordinances, as those which are for edification ; but there are also promises of converting grace made to them.

It was to church members that these promises were made, " The Lord thy God will circumcise thy heart, and the heart of thy seed to love and fear the Lord. And a new heart will I give you, and a new spirit will I put within you," &c. with many others which need not be repeated. And accordingly we find the church praying for converting grace, and thus pleading : " Turn thou me, and I shall be turned, for thou art the Lord my God ;" taking encouragement from their covenant relation to God, of which they were well assured, as being his visible people, however they might doubt whether their hearts were truly turned to him.

Besides, not only the more common ordinances and means of conversion are appointed especially, and chiefly, though not exclusively, for the benefit of church members, as they may need them, but there are some ordinances appointed peculiarly for the humiliation and conversion of such ; I mean the ordinances of church discipline, admonition, suspension, excommunication. These are designed as means to bring offenders to repentance ; and none but church members are to have these means used with them. So that it is not absurd or unreasonable that means of conversion be provided, in case of need, for those who when admitted are not known to need them.

Can

---

* On the church membership of Children, p. 3—4.

Can any good reason be given why means of conversion may not be appointed for orderly church members, who may need converting grace? Or why the word and sacrament may not be designed as means for this end, as well as that censures should be appointed for disorderly members, to humble them and bring them to repentance? Or must orderly members alone have no means of conversion provided for them?

Though none may come, or be admitted to the communion of the church, who are known to be unconverted, none but such as have and hold forth credible evidence of sanctification; yet some who according to the gospel rule have a warrant to come, and a right to be admitted, may not be true saints, and so may need converting grace as much as any. It is therefore, I think, so far from being absurd and unreasonable to suppose that the ordinances of the church may be designed and adapted to convey converting grace to those who need it, that this seems more to display the wisdom and goodness of Christ, that he has provided means for conveying the blessings of his grace to his covenant people according to their several needs, and makes the same means effectual to different ends.

If a hospital were erected, into which none were to be received but those who appear to be in health, yet since men have sometimes dangerous disorders upon them which are not known, it would be wise and kind to have provision made for the cure of such maladies, as well as for the maintenance of those who are well; and that, so far as might be, such a regimen be prescribed as might suit both those intentions.

It is further objected. If the Lord's supper be a converting ordinance, then it is so either to those only who think themselves godly when they are not so, or for such also as are sensible that they are ungodly. But it is not appointed a converting ordinance to either. Not to the former, because they who think themselves converted cannot use it as a means of conversion. Nor to the latter; for it would be absurd to suppose that men should be required to make a lying profession of piety as the means of their becoming real saints. To this I answer—

1. That the disjunction is to be denied. There are many who neither think themselves to be godly when they are not, nor are sensible that they are ungodly, but are in doubt respecting their spiritual state. Perhaps this may be the case with a great part of regular church members.

The Lord's supper may be a converting ordinance to such of these as are unconverted, notwithstanding what is here objected, which does not concern them.

2. A

www.ingramcontent.com/pod-product-compliance
Lightning Source LLC
Chambersburg PA
CBHW020123170426
43199CB00009B/615